HARRY POTTER THERAPY

HARRY POTTER THERAPY

AN UNAUTHORIZED SELF-HELP BOOK FROM THE RESTRICTED SECTION

Janina Scarlet Ph.D.

Illustrations by Vince Alvendia
Content Edited by Justin Zagri
Copyedited by Alan Kistler

This publication has not been prepared, approved, licensed, or sponsored by J.K. Rowling, her publishers, Warner Bros. Entertainment Inc., or otherwise any entity involved in creating or producing *Harry Potter* or the associated books or films

This book is not a replacement for mental health counseling and would ideally be used in conjunction with mental health support.

Copyright © 2017 Janina Scarlet Ph.D.
All rights reserved.
ISBN: 1548107158
ISBN-13: 9781548107154

To J. K. Rowling for bringing *Harry Potter* into our hearts and teaching us that love is the most powerful source of magic

CONTENTS

Introduction to the Wizarding World · · · · · · · · · · · · · · · ix

Part I	The Basic Rules of Magic · 1
Chapter 1	Suppressing Your Magical Potential · · · · · · · · · · · · · · 3
Chapter 2	Establishing Your Magical Identity · · · · · · · · · · · · · 12
Chapter 3	Mindfulness: The Protego Charm · · · · · · · · · · · · · · · 27
Chapter 4	"You're a Wizard" Accepting Your Magical Fate · · · · · · 41
Part II	Defense Against the Dark Arts · · · · · · · · · · · · · · · · 55
Chapter 5	Dumbledore's Army: Vulnerability Charm · · · · · · · · · 57
Chapter 6	Self-Compassion Transfiguration · · · · · · · · · · · · · · · 71
Chapter 7	The Defusion Incantation · 90
Chapter 8	Looking for your Values in the Mirror of Erised · · · · · · 99
Part III	Defeating Voldemort · 107
Chapter 9	Committed Action: Facing Your Inner Death Eaters · 109

Chapter 9¾   Mischief Managed – Mapping Out Your
            Magical Journey · 119

            References · 131
            About the Author · 137

INTRODUCTION TO THE WIZARDING WORLD

Dear witch or wizard,

Have you read and re-read the *Harry Potter* books? Are you someone who can quote the movies by heart? Do you still wonder when you will get your acceptance letter into Hogwarts School of Witchcraft and Wizardry?

Me too.

As a die hard and proud Potterhead, my heart warms every time I hear the film score *Hedwig's Theme*. I too, like many of you, have been sorted on Pottermore (House Slytherin) and have my own wand (Willow, 10-inch unicorn hair) and robes. For me, the *Harry Potter* series has been life-changing.

I picked up the first book *Harry Potter and the Philosopher's Stone* when I was in graduate school, shortly after one of my close friends lost a battle with cancer. I couldn't understand how people around me could be smiling and laughing when my heart was breaking. Didn't they know that I was dying inside, that everything felt meaningless and hollow?

I picked up the first book, wanting desperately to get lost in a world that wasn't real, away from my pain and from my feelings. The actual experience of reading these books was unlike anything I could have ever imagine before then. Instead of running away from my emotions, I came face to face with them. By immersing in the books, I found myself staring directly at my own Dementors of depression, my own grief and devastation, not unlike what Harry felt when he lost his godfather, Sirius Black, or his school Headmaster, Albus Dumbledore.

By reading these books and watching the films, I was able to both grieve over my loss, as well as learn how to cope with it.

Years later when I became a clinical psychologist, I started incorporating fictional characters from superhero comics, books, TV shows, and video games into therapy to treat patients with anxiety, depression, and posttraumatic stress disorder (PTSD). I was fortunate to be able to write on this topic for several anthology books, as well as my own book *Superhero Therapy*. However, I also always wanted to write a book specific to my favorite fandom, the one which undoubtedly influenced me the most. I decided that I would like to write a self-help book for my fellow *Harry Potter* fans to help them better manage their anxiety, depression, trauma, insecurity, and other difficulties. I hope that you will join me on an enchanting exploration of how the *Harry Potter* series can help us heal and find the magic in our own lives.

PART I

THE BASIC RULES OF MAGIC

CHAPTER 1

SUPPRESSING YOUR MAGICAL POTENTIAL

"Numbing the pain for a while will make it worse when you finally feel it."

- ALBUS DUMBLEDORE, *HARRY POTTER AND THE GOBLET OF FIRE*

WHEN HARRY POTTER, "the boy who lived," is only one year old, he is targeted by the evil dark wizard, Lord Voldemort. His only crime against the "Dark Lord" is Professor Trelawney's psychic prediction that either he or Neville Longbottom, another child, will destroy Voldemort. After his parents, Lilly and James Potter, die to protect Harry from Voldemort, Professor Dumbledore, Headmaster of the Hogwarts School of Witchcraft and Wizardry, sends Harry to live with Lilly's relatives, the Dursley family - Aunt Petunia, Uncle Vernon, and Cousin Dudley. Petunia and Vernon are aware that Harry will likely share his parents' magical talents, but they are highly critical and wary of magic, and preoccupied with being "normal." As a result, they try to keep their lives safe and predictable by hiding the truth from Harry, hoping he'll never discover his abilities or his true origins.

Many of us might try to suppress our own emotions in a similar way as the Dursleys suppressed Harry's magic without even realizing it. We might try to suppress the very thing that makes us magical - our emotions.

That's right, our emotions make us magical.

The practice of emotion suppression can have devastating consequences on a child. In *Fantastic Beasts and Where to Find Them*, we learn that magical children who have been physically or emotionally abused, or forbidden from using their magical skills at all, can develop an *Obscurus*, a parasitic magical force. This force will live inside the child and in turn make them an *Obscurial*. Obscurials constantly struggle to manage their emotions, experience mental breakdowns, and, in worst-case scenarios, die before they've reached the age of ten. This serves as a great metaphor for how our emotions work in real life. The more we suppress them, the stronger and more destructive they might become.

If we were to accept, even for a moment, that our emotions are what makes us magical, then we would need to learn how to use and properly apply our magical skills. Witches and wizards aren't born with instruction manuals. In fact, they have to learn specific spells, potions, enchantments, and transfigurations. Consider this book to be your own personal library of magic textbooks, not unlike those Hermione Granger would have checked out from the Hogwarts library.

Some Muggles and even certain magical folk are afraid of magic and might try to suppress it in themselves or others. They might even shame others for talking about our magical emotions or offer advice they believe to be helpful, but which tends not to be.

For instance, you might have been told some or all of the following by a Muggle or a well-meaning but misinformed witch or wizard:

- "You are too sensitive!"
- "Stop crying!"
- "You take everything so personally!"
- "Just stop thinking about it."
- "It's *just* anxiety."
- "Just get over it."
- "Other people have it worse than you."

Please check off or note the statements above that reflect what you've been taught. Feel free to write down others. Notice that in some ways, these statements might be similar to what the Dursleys do to Harry to suppress his magic. He is not even allowed to talk about his dreams.

The Dursleys are threatened by Harry's magical background, choosing to punish him for any seemingly abnormal behavior and electing to destroy his first acceptance letters to Hogwarts. Similarly, many people in our lives might feel threatened by emotional magic. Some people might punish, shame, or criticize us for expressing our feelings. Some bullies might have even called you a "freak" or "crazy" for being different, for being sensitive, for possessing your gift.

Unfortunately, most attempts to control and avoid emotions usually backfire in the long-term. For example:

Struggle	Strategies to manage it	Short-term Consequence	Long-term Consequence
Dursleys fearing that someone will find out about Harry's magical abilities	Hide Harry, yell at Harry, shame Harry, keep him misinformed about his heritage, lie about his parents' deaths	The Dursleys feel relief and believe that they appear "normal" to others in Little Winging	Harry keeps accidentally making magic happen in the worst possible times, such as at the zoo, for example
Dursleys trying to prevent Harry from receiving his letter	Trying to destroy the letters, bolting the mail slot, driving to a faraway location	The Dursleys feel relieved that Harry didn't get his letter, temporarily reduced fear	Hagrid shows up, explains everything to Harry and gives Dudley a pigtail
Mary-Lou Barebone tries to suppress magic in kids	Abuse and public rallies	Fear and obedience in children	One of her adopted children, Credence, develops an Obscurus and kills her
Ministry of Magic trying to deny that the Dark Lord returns	Propaganda posts in the Daily Prophet, trying to get Harry discredited	The public largely believes the Ministry	Voldemort comes to power and the Death Eaters take over the Ministry of Magic

As you can see, the Dursleys', the Ministry's and Mary Lou Barebone's very attempts to control situations, which made them uncomfortable ultimately backfired in the long-term.

Many Muggles, as well as a number of magical people might believe that emotions are "wrong" and choose to avoid them at all costs. Sometimes seeing other people struggling with anxiety can make the person witnessing this event feel anxious and even frustrated. This is often due to the potentially self-inflicted pressure to "fix" or control how other people feel. When they cannot fix how other people feel, these individuals are likely to become anxious and irritable, making them insensitive to the needs of others.

Now it is your turn to write down your own strategies that you have used to battle your own monster(s). Some of the strategies you have tried might have been helpful to you in both the long and short term (meaning that you no longer struggle with those difficult experiences), which is great! Some of them, however, might not have been as helpful. In order for us to figure out what is helpful and what isn't, let's fill out the table on the page below and look at the patterns. It is often helpful to see everything written out so that the patterns become clearer. You may be surprised at what you will find.

To begin this quest, we need to examine the struggles that you are currently facing. These are the monsters, which may be preventing you from leveling up in life or going on the kinds of quests that you would like. Maybe you struggle with overwhelming anxiety, debilitating depression or a painful loss. Perhaps you've had a major life change, or you or someone you know has been diagnosed with an illness. Chances are that, just like Harry, you might be facing several enemies at once, with many or most seeming too difficult to handle.

It is also possible that you have been facing these Dementors, Boggarts, or Death Eaters completely on your own or without proper weapons, armor, or enchantments. So, before we begin this quest, let's take an inventory of the current monsters (i.e., struggles) you are facing, the strategies you've used to manage them, and the short and long-term consequences of using these strategies.

Struggle	Strategies to manage it	Short-term Consequence	Long-term Consequence

What did you notice? Which strategies have been helpful and which have not? If you have some strategies that work, that's great! We call these "working strategies." Chances are that some of the strategies you've used to avoid the negative experiences of anxiety or other emotional pain have not been very effective in the long term. These are "non-working strategies." This is a common experience for everyone. As human beings, it is in our nature to find ways to avoid things that are unpleasant. Sometimes avoidance is helpful and necessary. For example, it made sense for Harry to hide from his abusive cousin Dudley and his bully friends. However, as we saw in most of the examples above, sometimes avoidance can lead to worse outcomes in the long-term.

After looking at the table above, it's easy to see that most strategies people use to try to control someone or something that cannot be controlled in that way, ultimately do not lead to healthy consequences. People's very attempts to control their emotions by trying to "just get over them" might make their situation worse. Contrary to what we might have been told, emotion expression is important and necessary for the proper development of our magical skills. People who told you that you need to "be strong" by hiding away and suppressing your emotions were, in fact, wrong.

I was always "the sensitive one." I remember when my father sat me down when I was nine years old and told me that my friend's mother passed away. I cried for several weeks. My family and friends were surprised by how much my friend's mother's death affected me. "After all, she was not *your* mother," they kept saying.

I connected to people and fictional characters on a deep personal level but struggled with small talk and what seemed like shallow conversations. I remember being at a friend's birthday party when I was ten years old, feeling really uncomfortable with other kids talking about which boy was cute and which girl was "a bitch." I sat back, watching the interaction around me, wanting to fit in, feeling so awkward. Feeling *different.*

And then it happened. One of the girls, "Mary," turned pale.

"I don't feel good," she said with tears in her eyes before running outside. I ran after her, as did the other girls. Mary was hunched over the railing, throwing up.

"Eww!" two of the girls screeched. Mary looked at them, pale and embarrassed. She tried to stand to run away but had another bout of vomiting.

I ran inside. I knew what to do. My mom used to do it for me when I used to get sick. I grabbed a glass of mineral water, napkins, and a wet towel and ran back out. Mary was sitting on the ground now, shaking and crying. The other girls had abandoned her because she was "gross."

"Go away!" she said, crying. "I'm gross."

"What?" I asked. "Don't be ridiculous. Here, let's get you cleaned up."

I helped her clean up her hands and put the wet towel around her neck. Then I handed her the mineral water to settle her stomach.

"Thanks," she said and then added, "I threw up."

"I know," I said. "It happens. And it happens to me too."

"That was so embarrassing," she said.

"Nah, it happens to everyone."

She smiled. We both felt perfectly imperfect and that was okay. I no longer felt awkward at that party. I felt connected.

In reading *Harry Potter and the Philosopher's Stone,* I could really relate to Harry feeling alone most of the time. I remember feeling this way, even when I was with my family, even when there were other people around, even in a crowd. I was different and I was told that my differences were strange and unacceptable.

So was Harry.

It isn't until Harry was eleven that Hagrid tells him, "You're a wizard, Harry." I was fifteen. My Hagrid, my message that I was special, appeared in the form of the first *X-Men* movie. In that story, I saw that super-powered mutants, people hated for being genetically different from others, were actually more evolved to be able to help others.

I later thought, what if empathy, sadness, anxiety, and depression are actually superpowers or magical abilities? What if the very things we are told that we need to suppress are ones we need to develop, grow, and accept? And what if I'm not the only one out there that's ever felt different, that's ever felt like they don't belong?

So, I must ask, dear fellow magical being, did you ever feel *different?* If so, when did you know that you were different? Did you ever feel like you couldn't fit in or had to hide who you truly are? What if what you're most ashamed of is the very thing that makes you magical?

And so, today I am honored to present to you your very own acceptance letter:

Dear Magical Being,

I am pleased to inform you that you have a place in this enchanting world where you are loved and accepted for the magical person that you are.

Your journey begins today, so be sure to jot down the date.

Yours sincerely,

Dr. Janina Scarlet,
Witch Psychologist

CHAPTER 2

ESTABLISHING YOUR MAGICAL IDENTITY

"I am what I am an' I'm not ashamed. 'Never be ashamed,' my ol' dad used ter say, 'there's some who'll hold it against you, but they're not worth botherin' with."

- RUBEUS HAGRID, *HARRY POTTER AND THE GOBLET OF FIRE*

THE FIRST SET of characters we meet in *Harry Potter and the Philosopher's Stone* are the Dursleys. Uncle Vernon specifically disapproves of anything out of the ordinary, including imagination and magical dreams, while Aunt Petunia forbids everyone from bringing up her deceased magical sister, Lily. The Dursleys have established an identity of *normal*, in their case meaning magic-free and inconspicuous. Magic is shameful to them. They're so desperate to fit in and so terrified of the truth being discovered Trying to maintain this *normal* identity causes them to have to lie to their families (Aunt Marge, for example), as well as friends, neighbors, and Uncle Vernon's potential clients. They say that Harry is "disturbed" rather than admit that he is a wizard. His magical heritage means that Harry, since his first arrival into the house at the age of one, is ostracized into the categories of "different" and "abnormal" by the Dursley's, and even bullied by his own family.

According to *social identity theory*, people's identity and self-concept can be influenced by the group they belong to (their *ingroup*, which in the case of the Dursleys would mean non-magical people).

Furthermore, a person might feel threatened by the members of the *outgroup* (a group with which they do not identify, such as the members of the magical community in relation to the Dursleys). The more strongly the person identifies with the members of their in-group, the stronger their sense of *ingroup favoritism* (a tendency to favor one group) will become, and the stronger their sense of *outer group derogation* (discrimination or belittling of the outer group) might be.

The Dursleys aren't the only ones who demonstrate strong in-group favoritism and outer group discrimination. Aunt Marge, Uncle Vernon's sister, also favorites Harry's cousin, Dudley, and despises Harry even though she does not actually know that he is a wizard. Aunt Marge treats Harry worse than her own dogs, often insulting his heritage and bullying him.

Just like the Muggles listed above, the wizarding community also has their fair share of in-group favoritism. Professor Severus Snape, who was previously bullied by Harry's father, James, and his friends in House Gryffindor, develops a strong dislike for Harry and other Gryffindors, while tending to favor students from the same house he belonged to as a student – House Slytherin. In Harry's year, a Slytherin student, Draco Malfoy, calls Harry's friend and Gryffindor classmate, Hermione Grainger, a *Mudblood*, a derogatory word for a Muggle-born magical person.

Draco Malfoy is an example of learned prejudice. The Pureblood families (where wizards are produced from two wizarding parents), like the Malfoys, do not accept Muggles nor witches and wizards who are Muggle-born (meaning one or both parents is a non-magical human). Taking things further than name calling, the biggest villain in the series, Lord Voldemort, argues to his followers the Death Eaters that all Muggles and Muggle-borns should be exterminated, despite the fact that his own father was a Muggle. In his case, his desire to fit in the wizarding community seems to have caused his hatred of anything related to Muggles. It seems that in trying to fit into their ingroup, some people might resent and bully the people from their perceived outgroup, often out of fear of not fitting in or due to the lack of understanding diversity.

V. Nigel Taylor, an American Snape cosplayer, best known as Vladimir Snape, accounts for his own experiences with being bullied in this way.

Nigel's Story:

I never fit in. I was abandoned at two years of age, having been left in the care of my paternal grandparents. I was raised in southern Indiana. Farm country.

It was high school where the differences were becoming more and more noticeable. I hadn't fit in for a long time, but I kept my head down. In those days, we were sat alphabetically in the class. My last name afforded me a seat in the back-left corner of the room in almost every class. I was invisible.

At sixteen years old I shaved the sides of my head and dyed the rest bright blonde. I nullified my own superpower. I was on the radar like a giant blimp. I stood over six feet tall already. Tall, skinny, and insecure. And quite visible. No longer able to slink into the shadows. I was walking in my own blond new wave spotlight.

My insecurities had been brewing all my life. My adoptive parents were convinced I'd be my father all over again. They didn't understand me. And at times tried to eliminate my creative side. I was told countless times I was going to grow up to be just like him.

He committed suicide when I was twelve. He was thirty-two. I lived with a fear that I wouldn't live past thirty-two years old.

I was told I was a "failure" at home and had the majority of my classmates telling me I'm "weird." They called me "gay" in a variety of words, none of which were polite. I dated a girl but that didn't matter. Maybe "faggot" was just another way to say weirdo?

I was chased, shoved, hit, chastised, and bullied for years.

Few saw it. And no one stepped in.

Nigel's story is all too common. I too was bullied in school, the worst of it in 7th grade. I was born in Ukraine and at the age of three was exposed to a large amount of radiation from the Chernobyl disaster. As a result, my health is forever compromised, and certain situations, such as weather and atmospheric radiation changes, cause me an immeasurable amount of pain. When I was twelve years old, my family and I immigrated to the United States as refugees to escape the violence and persecution that was taking place in my home country. Many of my American classmates did not understand what radiation exposure meant and as a result, many would joke that I was "radioactive" or "contagious." Many would ask me if I glow in the dark (I don't... yet).

Reading the *Harry Potter* series, I related to Harry's experiences of being ostracized in both in the Muggle world and in the wizarding world. For example, Harry prior to his attending Hogwarts, Harry is severely bullied by Dudley and his cronies in the Muggle world. When he attends Hogwarts, some of the students there ostracize him as well. For instance, in Harry's second year, many Hogwarts students believe that Harry is the heir of Slytherin, one of the four founders of Hogwarts, who is believed to have hated Muggle-borns. The rumors about Harry's supposed heritage spread throughout the school and many students fear, bully, or avoid him. Similarly, in his third year, Harry encounters the Dementors, horrible creatures that feed on people's painful memories and can suck out someone's soul. Harry, who experienced a lot of tragic losses and abuse in his thirteen short years at that time, has a strong aversive reaction to the Dementors – he faints when they get too close to him or when there are too many of them. This is the perfect ammunition for Draco Malfoy, who uses Harry's reaction to the Dementors as another excuse to bully him.

Although Harry is bullied before and even during his attendance at Hogwarts, he is able to establish his own identity over time. Specifically, rather than to buy into the public labels of him being somehow "weird," "dangerous," or "evil," Harry is able to focus on who he really is: *Harry*, a boy who enjoys playing Quiddich, someone who appreciates his friends, and likes Butterbeer. Sure, he acts out sometimes, as does everyone else. But his ability to speak the snake language of Parseltongue like the ancient wizard Slytherin does not mean that he is the Slytherin heir. Similarly, his most popular labels, "The Chosen One" or "The Boy who Lived" do not represent all of who he is. He is so much more than those two labels. He is the combination of some of them, as well as many others.

When we find our identity, beyond the society or self-prescribed labels, we can grow into ourselves. This is what happened to Nigel:

I hated my birth name. I legally changed my name when I was nineteen. Best thing I ever did. I changed my name to emulate Dracula and Duran Duran. Had Harry Potter *been released when I was a young teen, I'd be Snape. There's no doubt.*

I connected with Professor Snape immediately. Dark dry wit, steady sarcasm. Traits I know all too well. A past of being poor, and not belonging. A loss that I didn't share. That so few even knew.

Harry and I were a little alike. My biological father, Ronnie, was essentially Sirius Black. I got to know Ronnie a bit. When I was ten, we built a model together. He'd drive me to the local ice cream shop. He drove a muscle car and had long curly dark brown hair. It was like having a magical big brother. (His parents are the ones that adopted me). Then he died. Committed suicide. And just like Sirius through the veil, he vanished. My one connection to my family, that made me feel less a stranger, was gone.

I became a Snape cosplayer by accident. I had no intention at all of dressing up like the potions master for more than one film premier.

At Harry Potter conventions, I drew crowds. Lines. And people young and old wanted to talk to me.

I attended a panel at a HP convention in Chicago. There was a panel on Lily Evans Potter. It seemed a good thing for me to attend.

After being in the packed room for nearly fifteen minutes and no presenter... I stood up and in my best Rickman voice I said "I believe I am qualified to talk about Lily."

The room went nuts.

The following year I did a panel. My first. I expected twenty people. Over five hundred showed up. The first question I was asked was about bullying. They wanted to know how I felt about Peter and Remus. Since they were usually in the background and it was mostly James and Sirius that taunted and abused me. How did I feel about them? And so it began.

I answer questions in panels in the first person. And I now focus on Anti-bullying and Equality. Professor Snape became my super power. The world of Harry Potter has given me a much better gift than my invisibility I gave up so long ago. I could now talk to children of all ages and help them. Give them hope.

"Since Snape was both a bully and bullied," said Alan Rickman to my drummer at a play in New York City, "he uses that to talk to people." He seemed pleased to know I was using a character he portrayed in such a positive way. Knowing this makes me feel very good.

I don't carry a lot of the pain and isolation I felt throughout my formative years. I'm glad to say it's far less a weight than it once was. I'm not ashamed of it either. I can use it to connect with people. I'm able to relate. Fans of Harry Potter *that connect with the character of Professor Snape open up and talk to me freely about gender equality, bullying, unrequited love, and personal loss. I relate as best I can. Offering my advice as Snape. In short sentences with irregular pauses.*

J.K. Rowling has empowered me to be better version of me. I'm more vested in all that I meet. It's turned my empathy into a skill and not just an unruly trait. It's turned my painful past into a instrument of healing. I'm sarcastic and caring. Dark and filled with hope.

I'd like to think I'm doing it right.

BECOMING YOUR MAGICAL SELF

> "It is our choices, Harry, that show what we truly are, far more than our abilities."
>
> - DUMBLEDORE, *HARRY POTTER AND THE CHAMBER OF SECRETS*

In connecting with Snape and his musical interests, Nigel was able to find himself. He was able to find who he is and what he wants to stand for. He was able to recognize that he is more than his experiences. More recently, the *Harry Potter* series helped Nigel overcome his biggest struggle yet. In July 2017 Nigel was diagnosed with cancer. The night before his surgery he was understandably nervous and overwhelmed. In watching *Harry Potter and the Deathly Hallows,* Nigel reported a strong connection to Dumbledore's message to Harry at the Platform 9¾. Nigel said, "It was exactly what I needed, exactly when I needed it." Dumbledore's wise words, such as, "The true master does not run away from Death. He accepts that he must die and knows that there are far, far worse things in the living world than dying," helped Nigel be better physically and mentally prepared for his surgery, as well as to accept the inevitability of the upcoming treatment.

Currently, Nigel describes himself as a cancer survivor. The labels we prescribe ourselves can affect us positively or negatively. Nigel's "survivor" label can be helpful in assisting him on his journey to recovery. This label has also been show to be helpful with people who've survived abuse, sexual assault, and other traumatic experiences. On the other hand, other labels, such as "I'm a loser," are obviously painful and potentially toxic in how they affect us. Others still, the ones that include the roles we play in the lives of others, might be more benign but may sometimes also not be helpful. For example, I am someone who was bullied, I am someone who struggles with my own Dementors of depression and my own boggarts of anxiety, I am a trauma survivor, I am someone who struggles with my weight, as well as with beliefs that I am not good enough, not smart enough, and not experienced enough; *an amateur*. At the same time, I am a daughter, a sister, a wife, a mom, a psychologist, a scientist, a speaker, a friend, someone who likes to dance, someone who likes to write. I am someone who is compassionate and outspoken about social change, and someone who loves cats.

Although they are usually not as painful as the self-prescribed labels, (for example, *"I am not good enough"*) the self- or society-prescribed labels can sometimes be maladaptive as well. For example, when we are around our families, even in adulthood, we might carry the "I am a son/daughter/child" label and in fact, might act accordingly. We might, for example, be more cautious, feel less secure in our actions and behaviors, and act differently than we would with our friends. In fact, we might adopt an entirely or partially new identity when we are in different situations. While this can at times be helpful, in terms of letting us adjust to the given situation, at other times switching our identity to try to fit into a social situation can be exhausting.

One of the reasons why this might be the case is because when we are in those situations, the prescribed label (e.g., *"I am a daughter"*) might imply certain actions, beliefs, and abilities. For example, for some women the label *"I am a daughter"* might mean that when they are around their parents, they are more likely to not express their opinions, believe that they are weak, small, and incapable, and act in accordance to the belief that they are not capable of standing up to their parents. In this case, these labels might dictate how we feel, how we think, and how we act in certain situations. However, being any of those labels is a very small part of who we think we are.

One way to reclaim our true self is to see ourselves as an observer of these labels rather than only being any individual label. Allow me to elaborate. Imagine that you are reading the *Harry Potter* books. You read about Harry's struggles, only you are not Harry. You read about the house elves, only you are not a house elf. You read about the Death Eaters, only you are not a Death Eater. You are not the characters in the book. You are neither the pages, nor the letters on the pages. You are the reader who is observing these experiences. Similarly, you are not one of your labels, you are someone who might have a connection to all of them, and above all, you are the wise observer of these labels. It is therefore up to you how you would like to act and identify with them.

When we remember who we are and what we stand for in all situations, we are more likely to find our magical identity and maintain it in most, if not all situations. Neville Longbottom is a great example of someone who might act the way others expect of him to his disadvantage. When he was a child, Neville's grandmother and the rest of his family believed that he would turn out to be a squib (a non-magical human born to magical parents). As a result, his family, presumably without meaning any harm to him, essentially prescribes a label of *"not a good enough wizard"* to Neville. Neville carries this label with him to Hogwarts and it affects his confidence. When he is around Professor Snape, Neville is more likely to make a mistake with his potions. However, his apparent lack of ability seems far less prevalent when he is around an encouraging teacher, such as Professors Lupin or Moody.[1]

When Neville is able to face his boggart (a shape-shifting creature, which takes the form of the person, concept, or creature that the individual is most afraid of), he sees Professor Snape. Seeing Snape usually triggers Neville's "not a good enough wizard" label to control him, making him feel inadequate.

After he is able to face his boggart, however, Neville appears slightly more confident. Over time, he pursues a newfound passion in Herbology, joins Dumbledore's Army (an unauthorized student club where members learn magic combat and defensive spells), stands up to Voldemort and the Death Eaters, and singlehandedly destroys the last magical artifact that keeps Voldermort alive. In doing so, Neville essentially combines separate pieces of his identity into one. Even when it's hard. Even when he's afraid.

Let's take a look at the table below, which shows Neville's separate self-labels and then all of them combined. After that, let's fill out the rest of the table for Harry, Hermione, and then for you.

---

1 Professor Moody was actually Barty Crouch Jr. on Polyjuice Potion.

	Neville	Harry	Hermione	You
Separate self-labels	Shy, quiet, clumsy, parents were tortured and are now disabled, afraid of authority, loyal friend, good at Herbology, willing to fight for what he believes in			
How characters combine them to become their magical self	Joins Dumbledore's Army, stands up to Death Eaters, stands up to Voldemort, & kills Nagini			

What did you notice? Are there pieces of your identity that you over-identify with more than others? Is it helpful or hurtful? In some instances, our self-labels (for example, a loyal friend) can help motivate us to take helpful actions. In other situations, labels, such as "2nd best" or "not good enough" for Ron, can be hurtful. For me, I often over-identify with the "I'm fat and unattractive" label. Growing up in a culture that puts a high pressure on being thin, I, like most girls I grew up with, never felt "thin enough" or "attractive enough." There were times when I physically punched myself in the stomach because I hated the way I looked. There were also times when I cancelled plans with friends because I was too ashamed of how I looked. The irony is that I would never judge anyone else based on their appearance or ability. However, when it came to me, the standards couldn't be too high.

In my case, the label I most identified with held me back from being me, from living the life I wanted. However, for Kat, a blogger, therapist, and contributor of the following story, finding her Slytherin identity also allowed her to find herself.

Kat's Story:

After I got married, I slowly started to put on weight, as I think is pretty common. But after my daughter was born, I gained weight more rapidly. This is something that did not happen overnight and there are a thousand different factors, but one of the main factors is that I always put myself last.

I was so busy taking care of all of my external responsibilities- making sure I was the BEST mother, the BEST wife, the BEST friend, the BEST therapist, etc., etc., that I forgot to take the BEST care of me that I possibly could. I didn't listen to my own advice to others- that if I didn't take care of myself, I couldn't do my BEST at anything.

I passed all of the usual indicators that make people take notice and take action- numbers on a scale, BMI, moving from regular clothes stores to plus sized clothes stores, taking medication for high blood pressure, taking medication for high cholesterol, seeing multiple family members go through major heart surgeries. None of those did the trick.

What really got me was that the pain in my lower back was so bad I couldn't do simple things like walk to the end of the block so my kid could ride her bike without excruciating pain. That and the humiliation I felt when I was too big to ride several of the rides with my daughter at Legoland. What got me is that my health was impacting my ability to fully engage in and enjoy the world with my daughter.

I felt powerless over this element of my life. I have never had a healthy relationship with food or exercise- not even when I was thin and LOOKED healthy. I have been very successful in many things in my life- but never that.

I felt afraid of change. And then one day in September last year, when I was trying to figure out WHY I couldn't get a handle on this, I said, "F**k that- You are a Slytherin. There is NOTHING you can't do if you put your mind to it."

And so, I did.

I called my doctor the next day and made an appointment. I have been taking medication to help, but more importantly, eating healthier and exercising. Little lifestyle changes that are becoming bigger. In five months, I have lost 40 pounds, which is great- but what is better is that I FEEL better. I have energy. I can do things again. I can walk miles now- much further than the end of the block. I enrolled my daughter and myself in martial arts classes. Last week I even started bringing my walking shoes to work with me in case I am able to slip away for a bit.

By taking care of myself, I am being a better mother, a better wife, a better therapist, a better friend- a better me- and hopefully one that will be around for a long time.

When I start to get frustrated or disappointed, I use a little self-talk and remind myself that I am a Slytherin- that I can do this. You just watch me. But- when I indulge- which I do on occasion and without guilt (this is a lifestyle I'm living- not a diet) don't even think about saying anything to me or raising an eyebrow.

Remember- I am a Slytherin- I will bite and I have sharp fangs.

So, whether you are a Gryffindor, a Slytherin, a Hufflepuff, a Ravenclaw, a pureblood or a Muggle-born, remember that you are the full picture, not your labels.

HENCE:

You are not your depression.

You are not your traumatic experiences.

You are not your weight.

You are not what people call you when they are bullying you.

You are not what you call yourself when you are criticizing yourself.

You are not the roles you play in social situations.

You are *you*:

Magical, beautiful, amazing, magical you.

And who you are is beautiful.

Who you are makes a big difference in this world.

You are stronger, more powerful, more talented, and more loved than you can ever know.

May you feel how loved you are.

May you feel how much of a difference you make in this world.

TRANSFIGURATION PRACTICE:

For your practice assignment, spend some time this week embracing and connecting with your magical identity. Notice any traps in which you are connecting with one label or another, and see if you can remind yourself of who you are as a whole, of your full magical self, which you can be anytime and anywhere.

CHAPTER 3

MINDFULNESS: THE PROTEGO CHARM

"Worrying means you suffer twice."

- NEWT SCALAMANDER, FANTASTIC BEASTS
AND WHERE TO FIND THEM

ON HIS ELEVENTH birthday, Harry visits the magical and hidden Diagon Alley for the first time. He finds himself wishing that he had eight more eyes. Everything around him – cauldron shops, owl emporiums, broom shops, Madam Malkin's Robes for All Occasions store, and of course, Ollivander's wand shop – are literally and figuratively magical to him.

The first time he tries to eat a chocolate frog on the Hogwarts express train with his new friend, Ron Weasley, Harry is not at all upset that the frog leaps out of the open window. Instead, he is mesmerized. He is engaged with his surroundings, wanting to learn and experience everything he can in the magical world.

On the other hand, Draco Malfoy, a Pureblood wizard raised by wizards, is so used to the wizarding world that he is not fazed or impressed by the magic around him. When Harry and Draco first meet, they are both being fitted for their Hogwarts uniforms at Madam Malkin's Robes shop. Harry's and Draco's experiences of being there could not be more opposite. Whereas Harry is curious and excited, Draco appears to be bored.

At the same time, Draco does not appear to be interested in Muggle life either. When he meets Hermione, he is not only disinterested, but appears disgusted with Muggle culture. In contrast, when Ron's father, Arthur Weasley, meets Harry, and later, Hermione, he is full of excitement and curious questions, such as, "What exactly is the function of a rubber duck?"

Seeing and experiencing our surroundings as if we are entering a new and magical world, as Harry does, is an example of *mindfulness*. Mindfulness is a type of a magic charm, which allows us to notice our internal and external experiences as they are happening, in that moment. For example, noticing the sensation of your breathing (the rising and falling chest or abdomen with each inhale and exhale), noticing the sensation of your feet as they are making contact with the ground, noticing the smell and the taste of the food you are eating, are all examples of mindfulness.

PETRIFICUS TOTALUS CURSE

In *Harry Potter and the Philosopher's Stone*, Harry, Ron, and Hermione attempt to sneak out of the Gryffindor dormitory when Neville Longbottom attempts to stop them. Hermione casts the Petrificus Totalus curse, temporarily paralyzing Neville. The curse causes its recipient's arms and legs to snap together, become stiff, and prevent that person from being able to move until the curse wears off. Petrificus Totalus can be quite useful and Harry, Ron, and Hermione use it multiple times to petrify enemy Death

Eaters. Newt Scamander, a famed magizoologist (someone who studies magical creatures) and author of the Hogwarts textbook *Fantastic Beasts and Where to Find Them*, also used this spell in order to avoid capture.

It seems that the Petrificus Totalus curse can be quite effective when we are facing an enemy. But what if we are the recipients of this curse? For some of us, our anxiety might become so intense that we might feel petrified by our fears. Like a magical curse, an anxiety or panic attack can bind us, restrict us, and make us feel as though we are not in control of our movements or actions. Our mind might go blank, we might feel as if we are unable to move, or do what is required of us.

Hannah Abbott, a Hufflepuff student in Harry's year, frequently seems to struggle with anxiety. In her fifth year, she gets so nervous about her O.W.L.s (Ordinary Wizarding Level exams) that she starts crying in the middle of her Herbology class, stating that she is "too stupid" to be able to take her them. Despite taking a Calming Draught potion, Hannah still feels anxious and feels paralyzed as a result, which contributes to her making a mistake in her Transfiguration final exam.

Like Hannah, Ron's mother, Molly Weasley also struggles with debilitating anxiety. Molly frequently imagines that her family members will be injured in horrible ways, which causes her to be anxious, or at times, angry with them if they make her worry. Mrs. Weasley even admits that she imagines her family members being hurt, injured, or killed every single day. In fact, when Mrs. Weasley comes across a boggart, a shape-shifting creature, which takes place of one's biggest fear, the boggart turns into dead members of her family.

Molly and Hannah are so worried about the future that they both struggle noticing their present moment experiences. In fact, most of the time, their current experiences are not anywhere near as catastrophic as their imaginations of their worst case scenarios. However, when they imagine what terrible catastrophes might occur, they might feel and even act as if those catastrophes are occurring at that moment.

The pain of our past agonizing experiences can feel as if we have been hit with this curse. Even if the curse itself was relatively short lasting, the effects it might have on our mind and body can be extensive. What can make this curse even more disabling is if we are re-experiencing the excruciating event as if it is happening right now. For example, in *Harry Potter and the Goblet of Fire*, Harry competes against classmate Cedric Diggory and others for the Champion title in the Triwizard Tournament. Harry and Cedric win the Tournament together when they both touch the Triwizard cup, but it's a trap that transports them to Lord Voldemort, who immediately orders his servant to "kill the spare." In a flash, Cedric is gone in a coldblooded murder and Harry experiences severe torture, barely escaping Voldemort and his Death Eaters several minutes later.

For a long time afterward Harry has flashbacks, nightmares, and pain, experiencing apparent symptoms of posttraumatic stress disorder (PTSD). He appears to feel overwhelmed and has a hard time communicating about how much he is struggling. It is as if he is hit with the Petrificus Totalus curse, over and over again. Many of the trauma survivors I work with describe their traumatic experiences in this way.

There is no timeline for healing from the pain of our past, meaning that there is no time period in which we are expected to heal. Some people heal faster; others continue to have symptoms for a long period of time. However, one way we can try to ease our current experiences is by practicing mindfulness. In this case, mindfulness would require that we notice that we are affected by the past experience but also to recognize that this event is not happening in the present moment.

When Harry is having flashbacks of Cedric's death, he experiences them as if they are happening right now, in the present moment. Our physiology is connected with our thoughts, where our thoughts can affect our physiology and vice versa. For example, when Harry thinks about Cedric's death, chances are that he also holds his breath or starts breathing shallowly, that he experiences his muscles tensing and his heart pounding in his chest as his body releases adrenaline. Although Harry cannot change what happened to him or to Cedric, he might be able to reduce the effects of this excruciating event through the Protego Charm.

MINDFULNESS - THE PROTEGO CHARM

The Protego Charm protects the caster against minor to moderate jinxes, curses, and hexes. Although it might not protect the caster against major curses, such as the Cruciatus curse, it may protect them from the effects of many of the past or future curses and hexes. In order to practice the Mindfulness Protego Charm, we can observe our internal or external experiences. My favorite "quick and dirty" version of the Mindfulness Protego Charm involves asking ourselves, "Where are my feet?"

It might seem like a silly question, but most of us tend to spend so much of our time worrying about our future or thinking about our past, that we might have a hard time noticing our present moment experiences. When we actively feel and acknowledge our feet[*] on the ground, we may

---

[*] If the sensation of the feet is not accessible due to a disability or for any reason, you can use the sensation of your hands or your mouth.

also notice that at the present time the feared or the awful situation is not happening (though if it is, seek immediate safety).

See if you can try that now. Ask yourself: "Where are my feet?" See if you can feel your feet as they are making contact with the ground, feeling grounded and connected with the present moment.

Now, ask yourself: "Right now at this very moment, am I safe?" (If you are not, seek <u>immediate</u> safety depending on the situation; call the police, go to a safe location, or seek psychiatric care).

These are examples of practicing the Mindfulness Protego Charm – noticing our body, our feet, or our hands, or our mouth, noticing whether we are safe, and seeing if we can study the qualities of our pain, physical or emotional. It is almost as if we are learning to see the world through Moody's magical eye or through Luna's sense of wonder.

Everything we do is an opportunity to practice mindfulness. For example, cleaning can be a mindfulness practice where we notice ourselves cleaning and connecting with this experience like Harry does when he is helping clean Sirius' house to set it up for the Order of Phoenix. Similarly, eating or drinking can both be examples of mindfulness practice. Think of Harry when he first arrives at Hogwarts and tries the food at the Great Hall after the Sorting Ceremony. He enjoys the taste of sausages, Yorkshire pudding, and a treacle tart. He also drinks pumpkin juice, and later, in his third year at Hogwarts, tries butterbeer for the first time.

Whether you are drinking butterbeer or your morning coffee, this is another opportunity to practice mindfulness – slowing down enough to truly taste the beverage you are drinking or the food you are eating, as if you have never consumed it before, as if it is truly magical. Try it and see what you notice. Many people report that food and drinks taste better when they slow down and consume them mindfully. Similarly, you can also slow down and mindfully observe our surroundings, whether you are looking at the floating candles, the enchanted ceiling, paintings, nature, or the furniture around you.

THE MAGIC OF MINDFULNESS

The benefits of mindfulness are quite extensive and its effects on the body have been studied for several decades. Specifically, regular mindfulness practice seems to help people improve their physiological functioning. When we are hit with one of the many possible curses that life might throw at us, we might experience a *fight-flight-or-freeze response,* where we might become overwhelmed and where our body might begin to produce adrenalin to prepare us to deal with the perceived threat. Sometimes the threat might be real, such as a car coming right at you, in which case you would need to jump out of the way. In this case, the fight-flight-or-freeze response could help you react faster in order to keep yourself safe.

However, most of the time, our fight-flight-or-freeze response occurs when we assume we are in danger but we might not be. For example, if someone does not respond to our message, we might assume that they are mad at us and, as a result, might become overwhelmed with anxiety. We might, for instance, in our mind review the past conversations we've had with this individual and wonder where we went wrong. In this situation our body might also produce adrenaline and other stress-related chemicals, such as cortisol. However, unlike the previous example, where once we jumped out of the way of a speeding car, we might feel safe, in this situation, we are likely to continue ruminating about what might have occurred, potentially making our body sick with worry.

In fact, chronic stress, and even more so, stressing about stress, has been shown to be associated with increased health problems, such as worse functioning immune system, increased risk for heart disease, irritable bowel syndrome, autoimmune diseases, high blood pressure, increased risk for certain types of cancers and diabetes, and increased risk for strokes. However, it is not the stress itself that is wreaking this much havoc in a Peeves-like manner. It is our *interpretation* that stress is dangerous, our unwillingness to notice what we are thinking and feeling, that ultimately makes us feel worse in the long term.

Stress itself is perfectly normal and expected. If we can take slow purposeful breaths while stressed, if we can observe what is happening to our body or our thoughts even when we are stressed, we might be better able to manage stress. Research actually shows that regular mindfulness practice can reduce stress and overwhelm, improve attention and concentration, improve mood, including reducing anxiety, depression, and trauma symptoms, as well as reduce mood changes and food/substance cravings in people with addictions. Mindfulness can also potentially help people with sensory processing disorders and PTSD to reduce the distress and overwhelm when they are overstimulated or triggered. Finally, mindfulness has also been found to improve overall physical health, and is linked with improved brain processing, the creation of new brain cells, and extended lifespan.

WAYS TO PRACTICE THE MINDFULNESS PROTEGO CHARM

There are no right or wrong ways to practice casting this spell. Mindfulness essentially refers to paying attention to our internal and external sensations as they are happening in the present moment.

There are many misconceptions about practicing mindfulness. For example, some people believe that in order to practice mindfulness they have to empty their mind. This is not true. Everyone gets distracted while practicing mindfulness. The idea behind practicing mindfulness is noticing when you get distracted and then allowing yourself to return to your practice.

In addition, some people believe that if they are "doing it right," mindfulness is supposed to be relaxing and is supposed to feel good. Although mindfulness can sometimes be relaxing, it might not always happen that way.

Finally, some people believe that in order to practice mindfulness they have to sit still with their legs folded in a lotus position for many hours. This is one way to practice. However, you can also practice mindfulness in doing any activities you are engaging in, such as:

- Noticing your feet/arms
- Looking at your surroundings as if for the first time
- Mindful eating or drinking as if you are tasting and smelling this food or drink for the first time
- Noticing the sensations of water or soap on your skin as you take a shower
- Noticing yourself breathing or using a breathing app, such as *MyCalmBeat*

- Listening to guided meditations or practicing with one of the scripts below
- Noticing yourself driving/being driven, noticing as you are cleaning, typing, texting
- Checking in with your body every time you check the time on your watch or cell phone. Notice if you are anxious, stressed, tense, hungry, or in pain; taking a few breaths to slow yourself down
- Intentionally slowing down your speech or walking pace

FLYING MEDITATION

Imagine yourself standing outside Hogwarts Castle, about to partake in Madam Hooch's flying lesson. It is a beautiful sunny day and you can feel your feet standing firmly on the ground. At this very moment, you are exactly where you should be – in your flying lesson. At this moment, you are not late for anything, you are not in the rush to get anywhere. You are exactly where you should be, doing what you should be doing.

Before you take off, we are going to do a brief scan of your body, from your feet up to your head, pausing to take a breath at each step, filling your body with levitating magic.*

Take a moment to connect with the sensation of your feet once more. Notice if they are warm or cold. Achy or rested. Take a slow breath in, filling your body with relaxing magic. Breathe out, allowing your feet to relax and settle.

Now bring your attention to your legs, starting at your ankles, then your knees, and thighs. Take a slow breath in, filling your body with

---

* People who may struggle with connecting with their physical sensations due to a disability or trauma can practice connecting with those parts of the body that are accessible or comfortable.

relaxing magic. Breathe out, allowing your legs to relax and settle. If you notice that your attention has shifted, notice your feet once more to bring you back to the present moment and then return to this exercise.

Now bring your attention to your back, starting with your lower back, then your middle and then upper back. See how your back feels today. Is it sore, tired, achy, or relaxed? Take a few slow breaths in, filling your body with relaxing magic. Breathe out, allowing your back to relax and settle.

Now bring your attention to your stomach. The stomach is where we hold a lot of our emotions. Take a few breaths to see how your stomach feels today. Does it feel tight, achy, nauseated, or empty? Take a few slow breaths allowing your back to relax and settle. Spend some extra time here, maybe placing your hands on your stomach in order to better connect with this exercise.

Now bring your attention to your chest. This is another area where we experience a lot of our emotions. Take a few breaths to see how your chest feels today. Perhaps place your hand or both hands on your heart center, as a gesture of love and compassion, just as Sirius does to Harry in *The Prisoner of Azkaban* film. See if your chest feels tight or open. Take a few slow breaths allowing your chest to relax and settle. Spend some extra time here, breathing in and out.

Now bring your attention to your shoulders, arms, hands, and fingers. Take a few moments to see how they feel today. Are they tight, sore, or achy? Or are they relaxed today? Take a few slow breaths allowing these areas to relax and settle.

Now bring your attention to your neck, jaw, forehead, and the top of your head. We carry a lot of our tension in these areas. Take a few moments to notice how they feel today. Then spend a few moments focusing on your breathing, allowing these areas to relax and settle.

Now bring your attention to your surroundings. Take a few breaths while quietly noticing what you can see. Don't judge the cleanliness of your room or the objects around you, just see with open curiosity, as if you have never seen these objects before.

Now take a few breaths bringing your attention to what you can hear. Don't judge these sounds as "good" or "bad," just listen to them, take them in as they occur around you.

Now once more bring your attention to your feet as they are making contact with the ground. See if you can imagine yourself mounting the broom, kicking off the ground, and gently rising up in the air. Feel the wind as it gently caresses your face. See the water below you. Hear the birds chirping all around you. Take a few moments to breathe and enjoy the scenery you are observing.

When you are ready, gently land your broom back on the ground. Feel the sensation of your feet making contact with the ground once more. And take a few more breaths to fully connect with the experience of being present.

CHECK-IN

What did you notice during this practice? Some people report feeling more relaxed after a practice like this, while others might report being more anxious, or feeling the same as they did when they started. In addition, some people might be fully engaged with this practice while others might struggle with paying attention. Whatever your experience was is perfectly okay, and however you felt is the right way to feel. I encourage you to continue this practice at least a few days per week and see what you notice in terms of your anxiety, stress, and physical and emotional pain.

HALLOWEEN FEAST IN THE GREAT HALL MEDITATION

Another way to practice mindfulness is to practice it with an activity we do regularly, such as eating. I am going to use an example of a pumpkin pasty here but feel free to practice it with any food you are about to consume.

First, take a few breaths, allowing yourself to feel the sensations of your feet as they are making contact with the ground. If at any time during this exercise or in the future you find yourself feeling distracted or overwhelmed, ask yourself "Where are my feet?" and feel the sensation of your feet once more. This will help bring your back to the present moment.

Now bring your attention to the food you are about to eat, such as a pumpkin pasty. Take a few moments to breathe slowly and rhythmically while you look at the pasty. Look at it as if you have never seen it before. Look at it with Luna-like curiosity. Turn it around, turn it over. Really study it.

Now bring your attention to how it feels to touch. Is it warm or cold to the touch? Is it sticky, soft, gooey, or firm in your hands? Take a few breaths here as you are practicing.

Now bring your attention to the smell of the pasty. Bring it up to your nose and smell it for a few moments while continuing to breathe. Notice if the smell of the pasty smells sweet or sour. Notice the sensations in your mouth as you smell the pasty. Is your mouth starting to water?

Now slowly bring the pasty up to your mouth and take a small bite. Just see what it tastes like without chewing it. Continue to breathe as you slowly begin to chew your pasty. How does it taste?

Take your time to finish the rest of the pasty in the same way. What did you notice? How does it taste compared to when you do not eat mindfully? Many people report that food tastes better and that they enjoy their food more when they practice mindful eating.

Quiddich practice: This week, look for opportunities to imagine that you are in Diagon Alley, learning how to play Quiddich, or are getting sorted into your House in your first year at Hogwarts. See if you can practice experiencing things around you as if for the first time, with Harry-like excitement, or with a Luna-like sense of wonder.

CHAPTER 4

"YOU'RE A WIZARD" ACCEPTING YOUR MAGICAL FATE

"Understanding is the first step to acceptance, and only with acceptance can there be recovery."

– ALBUS DUMBLEDORE, *HARRY POTTER AND THE GOBLET OF FIRE*

I STILL REMEMBER that morning. It was 9:25am. I was trying to sleep, having gotten home after 2:00am. My cellphone rang. It was my mother. I groaned and sent the call to voicemail. She called again.

"Hello?" I said, my voice still groggy.

"There was a terrorist attack on the Twin Towers. You can't go to the city today."

The words didn't make sense.

"Huh?" I said. "You don't understand, I have a job interview at noon at the Trade Center and then a rehearsal at two."

"You don't understand." Her voice sounded stern. "Two planes hit the Twin Towers. You can't go to the Trade Center. You can't go into the city."

I sat up. We didn't talk for several minutes. Neither of us knew what to say.

"Is Michael okay?" I finally asked, realizing that my brother worked not too far away.

"I haven't been able to reach him."

My heart hurt. I hung up with her and turned on the TV. I tried calling my brother. No answer. There were the Twin Towers, the very ones I just saw some twelve hours ago as I was taking the train back to Brooklyn. Only now they were covered in smoke. People were running out. Images and videos of the planes crashing into the buildings were playing on repeat. I tried Michael again. Still, no answer.

I got dressed and went up to the roof, which overlooked the Hudson River, on the other side of which stood the two tallest buildings of New York City. I stayed there for a long time, watching the smoke, watching them fall, as if watching some kind of a surreal movie. Feeling both numb and excruciating pain all at the same time.

My phone rang. It was my brother. He was safe and walking home along with thousands of others over the Brooklyn Bridge. I could finally sigh with relief.

I went back downstairs and watched the buildings collapse over and over and over again. I watched the people of my city, covered in soot, broken, covered in blood, helping one another in making it out of the rubble. Over the next few weeks, countless people went down to where the Twin

Towers stood, Ground Zero, helping others to look for loved ones, to offer support, and to assemble body parts.

I never went.

I felt so hurt and so broken by what had occurred, wishing that I somehow could have prevented it, wishing that I could have helped somehow, but all the same, feeling helpless and overwhelmed with debilitating grief. For several months, I did not speak of this event. I couldn't.

Yet, the more I tried not to think about it, the more I tried to suppress it, shut it down, push it away, the more the events of that horrific day haunted me in my daydreams and nightmares.

It wasn't until I started to actively participate in Creative Arts Team (CAT) Youth Theatre that I felt some relief. CAT Youth Theatre put together original plays written through improvisation by teens under the direction of NYU instructor Helen White. That year, the theme was obvious. Through improvisation, we created a play about 9/11. It was no longer possible to avoid my pain. I came face to face with it. I had to learn to face it, to accept it, and to embrace my pain in ways I could not begin to comprehend. During rehearsals, many of us began to share our own experiences, giving us a doorway for healing. Many of our audience members were families of the fallen firemen and other first responders, who came to watch the play, who cried with us, in unity, allowing us all to find the glimpses of light within the darkness of this tragedy.

Avoidance and suppression of our emotions will often lead to us expressing them in not the most helpful ways. In the case of Harry Potter, he understandably struggles with processing Cedric's death. In fact, most of his summer following this tragedy is quite atrocious. Harry is having nightmares and flashbacks about the way that Cedric died and he has no one to talk to. To make matters worse, when the Dementors attack Harry and Dudley, Harry is temporarily kicked out of Hogwarts for casting the Patronus Charm. Feeling alone and frustrated, he takes out his emotions on Ron and Hermione when he sees them. The anger and hurt inside him about what he had been through, about the Ministry of Magic not believing him or Dumbledore that Voldemort has come back to full power, enrages Harry. As a result, his friends are nervous to talk to him, worried that he will "bite their heads off." Not being able to process and discuss the events surrounding Cedric's death with anyone and not being able to vent about the Ministry's ignorance regarding Voldemort's return, causes Harry to push away the people closest to him. Thankfully, they stay by his side through it all.

PINK DEMENTOR: AVOIDANCE CREATES THE OUTCOME YOU'RE TRYING TO AVOID

Avoidance of our internal experiences (thoughts, memories, and emotions) often creates the very outcomes we are trying to avoid. Don't believe me? Let's try an exercise. I would like for you to picture a pink Dementor. Pink robes, pink hood, all pink and sparkly. Really focus on it for a few seconds.

Got it? Great! Now I would like for you to close your eyes for approximately one minute and to try everything possible to *not* think of the pink Dementor. Do **not** imagine the pink Dementor, do **not** think of the words "pink" or "Dementor" at all. Just push them away, erase them from your memory. Don't be shy now! Give it a go!

Check-in. How did that go? Most people report that they might be able to distract themselves in the short-term by focusing on something else or by thinking about something else but that in general the pink Dementor shows up, as if playing a creepy game of hide-and-seek with your mind.

Now, let's try the opposite. I would like for you to please close your eyes for approximately one minute and focus only on the pink Dementor. Think of nothing else and do not visualize anything else. Keep your full focus on only the pink Dementor. Ready? Go!

Check-in. How did it go? Most people report that after a little while they start to get bored and lose their focus, get distracted, or think about something else.

This is how avoidance works most of the time. Avoiding our thoughts and feelings can usually make them more intense in the long-term, whereas experiencing and facing them can make them less overwhelming over time. This applies to anxiety, depression, our worries about our appearance, and our traumatic memories. For example, like many people reading this book, many of my clients struggle with overwhelming depression. I myself have had days where it feels like I've been attacked by an army of Dementors while being hit with a Cruciatus curse. On these days, everything might feel heavy, hopeless, and bleak. In my case, I start to feel like there is a spreading emptiness in my gut, as if I have been stabbed repeatedly, only the physical pain has become so severe that it became numb. On those days it becomes impossible to enjoy the things I normally do, it becomes very difficult to function, and to support others.

Doing a simple task like answering a text message or an email becomes impossible. On those days, avoiding unpleasant tasks and feelings of impending doom might seem really appealing. We might binge on a Netflix series or distract ourselves with a book, a video game, or most often, our cell phone.

Sometimes a short break during which we engage with something we love can provide enough of a Patronus to help us feel well enough to get back to work. But at other times, we might continue binging on distractions, as well as snacks, drinks, or just about anything else so we can escape the terrible pain that we feel. The more that we fight it, the more we resist it, the worse we might feel.

Do you recall the Devil's Snare plant at the end of *Harry Potter and the Philosopher's Stone?* The Devil's Snare uses its vines to ensnare anyone it touches. The more you struggle against the Devil's Snare, the tighter its grip, which can ultimately be suffocating. Ironically, in order to escape the Devil's Snare, you have to "relax," which allows this enchanted plant to then relax its grip on you. Now, of course relaxing while you're being strangled might seem impossible, as might facing your Dementors of depression. However, the willingness to take one or several breaths while you're being entangled in the Devil's Snare might allow your body to become less tense, thereby allowing the plant to let go of you. Similarly, the willingness to acknowledge your depression Dementors might make them less overwhelming.

Acknowledging your depression, your anxiety, your thoughts, or your unchangeable predicaments has to do with the willingness to accept the fact that it is happening in the first place. Like receiving a Howler, a loud angry letter, we need to open and look into our emotions, before they explode. In fact, when Aunt Petunia receives a howler from Professor Dumbledore, Harry wisely reminds her, "Open it, it will happen anyway."

Psychologist and self-compassion researcher Kristin Neff states that the more we resist the pain that is already there, the more we increase unnecessary suffering. What this means is that we all experience some level of pain, both physical and emotional. Most of it is unavoidable, especially if we have a chronic condition, such as chronic pain, Multiple Sclerosis, Parkinson's, or reoccurring depression. However, the more unwilling we are to experience the pain that is there anyway, the worse we will actually feel. According to Neff, the formula for this is essentially –

Pain x Resistance = Suffering

In other words, the more we resist the unchangeable pain we are exposed to, the more we increase our suffering. On the other hand, the more likely we are to accept the reality of something that isn't going to change, the easier it might be for us to process this event. For example, Harry might hate the fact that he has to keep going back to live with the Dursleys every summer. However, the more he resists this fact, the more painful it becomes when he has to go back.

I remember the first time I talked to someone about *acceptance*, or the willingness to accept my emotions. I was 24, I had just lost a dear friend to cancer, and my therapist *dared* to say that I needed to work on acceptance of this event. I folded my arms and stared at her, thinking, *"You've got to be kidding, lady!"* I did not want to accept anything. Like Harry, after Sirius' death, I wanted to break things. I was angry. I wanted to scream about how unfair it was that she died, being so young, so full of life. The last thing I ever wanted to do was to accept that it really happened. Over time, however, I was able to understand what acceptance is and what it is not.

Acceptance is not	Acceptance is
Giving in	The ability to experience the emotions and sensations that show up in the given moment without pushing them away
Giving up	The willingness to understand that something cannot be changed, if it truly cannot, such as accepting *that* someone has died, or accepting *that* someone was hurt
Putting up with injustice or abuse	The willingness to recognize what can be changed (if anything) and stand up for what is right, such as bringing a perpetrator to justice, or to support ourselves and others in the time of grieving
Consenting to mistreatment or condoning immoral acts	The willingness to endure short-term distress for a larger picture of what is important to us, such as the willingness to finish our work because of the way it might improve our future or help others

HOW TO PRACTICE ACCEPTANCE

*"Rock bottom became the solid foundation
on which I rebuilt my life"*

- J. K. ROWLING

In her famous Harvard graduating address, *Harry Potter* author J. K. Rowling talked about her struggles. Just seven years after she graduated college, Rowling was going through a bitter divorce, she was unemployed, and was on the verge of homelessness. It was thanks to this setback that she began to pour all her energy into what she was really passionate about – her writing. Her life at this point was not easy, many of her struggles were excruciating. And, at the same time, her willingness to accept her circumstances and her willingness to endure rejection as she continued to write and submit her book to publishers ensured her long-term success as an author.

I imagine that for J. K. Rowling, acceptance practice included a lot of anxiety about sending out her manuscript, noticing this anxiety, breathing, and sending it out anyway. There is no one way to practice acceptance, we need to learn to become curious about our emotions and experiences, as if reading them in a book or watching them on the screen. The question then becomes whether or not you are willing to experience discomfort in order to see the bigger picture. Would you be willing to experience anxiety if it meant being able to spend time with people you care about? Would you be willing to feel the discomfort of depression if it means that you will get to do great things, like Harry Potter does?

When Hagrid finds Harry on his 11th birthday and tells him that he is a wizard, Harry does not initially believe him, thinking that there was some kind of a mistake. Harry was probably pretty anxious to trust Hagrid and to go to London with him, let alone attend Hogwarts. Imagine if Harry gave in to his anxiety. His story would probably go like this –

"You're a wizard, Harry."

"Umm, I don't think so. I don't feel good enough to be a wizard."

Voldemort comes back to power and kills Harry anywhere outside of the Dursley's house before Harry turns seventeen.

The End.

What if every time you feel too anxious or too overwhelmed to try something new, something seemingly difficult, you are actually turning away from your own magical journey. What if you are actually the chosen one, on your particular path, to make an extraordinary difference? This path, much like Harry's, will not be easy. It will be full of trials, including Boggarts, bullies, and Dementors. But what if on the other side of that is an important victory? What if on the other side of your comfort zone is where the magic starts? Would you be willing to take that chance then? Would you be willing to experience short-term discomfort if it meant that you get to be the magical hero of your own story?

Avoiding troubling thoughts, feelings, and events will not make them go away. Much like the Ministry of Magic's ignoring of Voldemort's return, we cannot change what may already be happening simply by ignoring it. But much like Harry, Ron, and Hermione, we might be able to make a difference by facing it head on.

Dumbledore himself reminds Harry that he needs to accept what happened to him in order to help him better cope with Cedric Diggory's death. Talking about Cedric's death with his friends helps Harry accept the reality of this tragedy over time. One of the people who help him feel "normal" is Luna Lovegood, an eccentric Ravenclaw girl who, like Harry, is able to see the Thestrals. The Thestrals are horrid-looking creatures, which can only be seen by those who have witnessed death.

I believe that the willingness to see the Thestrals after experiencing death is a multi-layered metaphor for what happens to those who experience a tragic loss. First, there is a potential invisible scar, not unlike the physical one Harry has on his head, one, which hurts at the reminders of the loss or a traumatic experience. Losses allow the survivors, like Harry, Luna, and Neville, to see things differently compared to people who might not have experienced a loss or a trauma. In some ways, people who experience losses and traumatic experiences might be more grown up, having a better understanding of death and loss. In other ways, they might still see the ones who have died around them, maybe wish to call them, maybe even pick up the phone, out of habit to call or text the person that has passed.

Additionally, the person who experienced a loss must be willing to see the Thestrals, willing to acknowledge and experience their loss in order to heal and recover. The truth is that the most difficult experience has already passed. You've already lived it; you've already been through the worst of it. By accepting that it did in fact occur, by facing it, you can heal from it. This is exactly what Yasmin did – by facing her harrowing traumatic experiences, she was able to not only heal from them, she became a true hero to others, much like Harry, Ron, and Hermione do.

Yasmin's story
I was eleven when I first read Harry Potter. It was 1999, and the first three books were already out. I was at my favorite bookstore when I saw there was a drawing contest. "Draw a scene from a Harry Potter book."

I flipped through the three sleeves and was most drawn to "Chamber of Secrets," so I bought it and read it through in a day or two.

I became instantly engrossed. And me being a small, bookish, smarty-pants girl with brown, bushy hair, larger front teeth, and brown eyes, I felt an instant connection with Hermione. I found a lot in common with Ron, as well. Being 100% Puerto Rican with all my family (but me) being born in Puerto Rico, I was from a truly "pure blood" family. Being the youngest of 9, and the daughter of a teacher and mechanic, I knew very well what it was like to grow up in a home that had much more love than money. We even all shared the same features - dark brown/black hair and brown eyes. Well, everyone except my mother. She had black hair, glasses, and the only member in my entire family that I knew of with clear, green eyes.

I won the drawing contest (the scene I drew was Dobby zapping Lucius Malfoy, for the record), and quickly bought the other books.

Then, a few months later, it happened. On January 22, 2000, my father (a man whom I had been immensely close with) killed my mother.

There were no red flags. They had argued a great deal while together, but had been separated for years. I learned that all of my older siblings wanted to put me up for adoption to not have to deal with me. Only three siblings wanted me. I chose to stay with my sister, Abby.

Not even a year later, I realized that was a mistake. I endured years of emotional (and, at times, physical) abuse at her hand. I had already been the victim of sexual abuse at the hand of one of my half-brothers when I was a child, so coupled with the other more recent traumas, I had become a seasoned veteran and handled it all "fine".

I loved school and it quickly became my refuge. I spent all day studying and doing homework. I looked forward to being with my school friends. School became my home. In my junior year of high school I took a psychology class and instantly knew that this was my calling. Every day after that point was me tirelessly working towards becoming an adolescent therapist, to help other kids like me. And this year will mark my first full year as a licensed mental health counselor with about four and a half years of experience working with adolescents.

It took me years before I ever really stopped to process and think about what happened to me. All of it. I think as a kid, it was all too easy to just bounce back from everything.

I cannot deny that those experiences have left an indelible mark on me. I see them now that I am older and wiser. I just thought I dealt with things better than everyone else, an ignorant, arrogant belief I no longer hold now that I understand the complex, multi-faceted way that grief and trauma can be experienced by individuals. I am proud of the work that I do with youth, and am currently writing an academic paper for the Harry Potter conference in Philadelphia.

I didn't ever actively read Potter as a refuge. I just thought that my love for it then was no different than my love for it before my parents died. But I think now that I can look back with clearer eyes, that the books did offer a form of therapy to me, even if I didn't know it at the time. I am forever grateful to the series for its protection over me, much like Lily's invisible love over Harry. I will always love the books immensely. Always.

Willingness practice: For this week's practice, make a list of feelings, thoughts, and events you tend to avoid. Start small. See if there is one or two you would be willing to try out.

Be creative in how you'd like to face these. If it's thoughts or memories you are avoiding, write them down, draw them, or say them out loud repeatedly until they start losing their power. If it's your emotions you are uncomfortable with, see if you can sit with your emotions for ten minutes to try to get to know them. If you can't do 10 minutes, do 5. Do something.

If it's a fear of judgment or a self-image issue that you are struggling with, see if you would be willing to do something small, like asking a question, making eye contact, or looking in the mirror for a few minutes. If it helps, think of it as an undercover mission for the magical community to determine how emotions work in the Muggle world. Observe and report back.

Would you be willing to give it a try if it means that you get to become a magical hero in your own story? Give it a shot. I believe in you.

PART II
DEFENSE AGAINST THE DARK ARTS

CHAPTER 5

DUMBLEDORE'S ARMY: VULNERABILITY CHARM

"This pain is part of being human . . . the fact that you can feel pain like this is your greatest strength."

— ALBUS DUMBLEDORE, *HARRY POTTER AND THE ORDER OF THE PHOENIX*

ON SEPTEMBER 1, 1991 Harry Potter sets foot at King's Cross Station on Platform 9¾ for the first time in his life. When he first gets to the station, he's unsure how to access the platform, but luckily runs into the Weasleys and asks for help. In order to get to Platform 9¾, Harry has to run through the wall between platforms 9 and 10. He needs to trust the magic and that he will not run into a solid brick wall.

The barrier at the Platform 9¾ was just one of the many barriers Harry had to overcome during his time at Hogwarts. Arguably one of the biggest barriers that stands in his way later is Professor Dolores Umbridge, a sadistic professor who physically and emotionally tortures students who don't agree with her or fall in line. She forbids students from learning the

Defense Against the Dark Arts Spells and suggests that they only need to read books to understand the theory behind the spells.

Realizing the danger of the Hogwarts students not knowing how to protect themselves against the Death Eaters outweighs the danger of getting in trouble with Professor Umbridge, Harry teaches Hogwarts students in secret, establishing "Dumbledore's Army." As with anything meaningful, forming this group creates a risk, in this case a risk of punishment from Umbridge. In fact, Harry and his friends did eventually get caught and did get in trouble. However, the willingness to take that risk in the first place, ends up saving many lives by ensuring that the students are later able to fight the Death Eaters.

The willingness to be open with our emotions is kind of like the willingness to join Dumbledore's Army. Sure, you might get hurt, but you might get hurt even if you are not willing to be vulnerable. You have more of a chance of getting what you want if you are willing to be vulnerable than if you are not.

Vulnerability researcher Brené Brown points out that the word "vulnerable" literally means "woundable," meaning that a vulnerable person is someone who is opening themselves up to the possibility of being hurt. You might ask, why would anyone ever want to take that chance? Why would anyone ever want to or be open to the possibility of being hurt? Wouldn't it be better to close ourselves up?

It turns out that emotions come in a packaged deal. We cannot selectively numb some emotions that we do not want to feel, such as fear, depression, and shame, and only feel happiness and joy. If we numb some of our emotions, we numb all of them. In fact, purposely suppressing our painful emotions makes it more likely that we might become depressed, have anxiety/panic attacks, and possibly even consider or engage in self-harming behaviors. Many of my patients who struggle with panic attacks are surprised to learn that they might have been avoiding grieving over a painful loss or trauma, their interpersonal frustration, or avoiding exploring their fear of death. All of these experiences are completely natural in that most of us don't want to think about our painful emotions and pretty much everyone fears their own mortality or the possibility of losing their loved ones. Voldemort himself is so afraid of death that he creates seven Horcruxes, objects in which he stores pieces of his soul to ensure he can later resurrect. The only problem with his plan is that each time he creates a Horcrux, Voldemort takes an innocent life. Each time he took a life, Voldemort split his soul. Each time he splits his soul, Voldemort becomes less and less human and less able to truly enjoy and experience the very thing he fights so hard to maintain – his life.

While numbing selective emotions makes it more likely that we will experience emotional (and sometimes, physical) pain, safely exploring our emotions can actually be a healing experience. In the Muggle world there are certain myths, which make it sound as if emotions are meant to be suppressed or are somehow a sign of weakness. Extensive neuroscience and psychology research has demonstrated these myths to be inaccurate.

<u>Here are some common myths and misconceptions about emotions:</u>

Myth #1. Emotions are a sign of weakness. This is a common myth, instilled in many people since a very young age.

Boys, for example, might be taught that in order to grow up to be "a real man," they are not supposed to cry, not supposed to be afraid, nor show their emotions in any way. They might even be shamed for being "like a girl" if they demonstrate emotions.

Girls, on the other hand, might be shamed for experiencing emotions as well. They might be told that they are "too emotional," "hormonal," or "too sensitive," for experiencing emotions. Whereas boys might be shamed for not being "man enough" for demonstrating emotions, girls might be shamed for being "too crazy."

In reality, research studies and clinical cases demonstrate that psychologically speaking, exploring and experiencing our emotions is the healthiest thing we can do for our mental health. I also argue that exploring our emotions is the most courageous thing of which humans are capable. To be courageous does not mean to be fearless. To be courageous means to be afraid and do what is important to us anyway, despite any fear that we might have. I have spent many years working with trauma survivors, including Veterans and active duty Marines, some of the most courageous people I have ever met. Many of them state that processing their emotions was far scarier and more intimidating than the atrocities they face in the war. The fact that they are willing to explore what they are most afraid of shows definite courage in their case. The fact that you might have at some point explored and experienced some very uncomfortable emotions in the past even though you were afraid, shows how courageous you truly are. Harry and Ron are undoubtedly scared when they go into the Chamber of Secrets. However, they go there in order to save Ginny, as well as Hermione and others who are petrified. In feeling their fear but not allowing it to deter them from what is important, Harry and Ron display true courage. Therefore, feeling emotions is not a weakness; it is the ultimate sign of strength and courage.

Myth #2. Feeling your emotions will cause them to become so extreme that you won't be able to stop and will keep feeling them forever. Research and clinical case studies show just the opposite – feeling your emotions might be uncomfortable at first but the more you allow yourself to feel and connect with your emotions, the easier it gets to do so over time. On many occasions, Dumbledore advises Harry to connect with his pain and emotions in order to heal from his past.

Myth #3. You are safer if you don't feel anything at all. Quite often I've seen just the opposite. People who numb their emotions have a more difficult time caring about themselves or others, connecting with others, and are more likely to engage in unsafe behaviors such as substance use or self-injury.

Myth #4. If you don't feel your emotions, they will go away. In *Harry Potter and the Prisoner of Azkaban,* we learn that the Dementors feed on people's painful memories and experiences. If we ignore our emotions, we might be less likely to be able to function when they do arise. Although Harry experiences more and more painful events as the series continues, his ability to withstand the Dementors gets better because he is more used to facing them and therefore knows how to manage them with the Patronus Charm.

Myth #5. You must feel happy at all times, if you don't there's "something wrong with you." All emotions, including happiness, sadness, depression, anxiety, and others, are temporary. It is true that some last longer than others. However, it is unrealistic to assume that we must feel happy all the time. Not a single character in the *Harry Potter* series is happy all the time. Harry, Ron, and Hermione experience a wide range of emotions – happiness, sadness, anger, anxiety, grief, hopelessness, and frustration, just to name a few. Even Dumbledore, arguable the wisest person in the series, experiences a variety of emotions.

Myth #6. Other people don't feel emotions that you feel and cannot relate to what you are experiencing. There are probably many reasons why you might like the *Harry Potter* series. There might have been something that spoke to you about some of the characters at some point. The truth is that our experiences are not unique in that many of us experience the exact same emotions and have similar thoughts. However, many of us might be too uncomfortable or afraid to talk about these. We might have been shamed or judged in the past and might therefore assume that others will be just the same. For example, Madame Maxime is so uncomfortable with talking about her giant heritage, assuming people will judge and reject her, that she lashes out at Hagrid for bringing it up.

However, Hagrid, of all people, knows what it is like to look different and be judged for it. This makes him more compassionate toward those who are singled out and bullied, such as when Draco bullies Hermione for being Muggle-born.

Myth #7. If anyone else finds out that you have the emotions or the thoughts that you feel, or got to know the *real* you, they would judge you, think that you are "crazy," never love you, and never want to be around you again. Harry's scar hurts when Voldemort is near him; he hears voices, has visions, and speaks

Parseltongue. There are times he does not want to tell even those closest to him about his symptoms, either because he does not want to worry them or because he fears being judged. I imagine that at no point did you ever judge him for these experiences when reading the *Harry Potter* books or watching the films. What if some people not only accept you for the *real* you but also love you because of it? What if knowing about your fears and insecurities actually makes you more endearing and loveable? In fact, the more we can learn to accept our own shortcomings, the more open we can be with others, the more loveable and open to love we are likely to become.

"Name it and you tame it. Feel it and you heal it."

- Psychology researchers Kristin Neff, PhD and Chris Germer, PhD

Dumbledore did not say the above quote, but he might as well have and would have been right. What he does say to Harry in *Harry Potter and the Philosopher's Stone* is, "Fear of a name increases fear of the thing itself." By naming our emotions, we may become less afraid of them. Often, we might feel more than one emotion at the same time. Naming each one of them, for example, depression, fear, hopelessness, and shame, can make it easier to manage them. Furthermore, allowing ourselves to become curious about and feel our emotions will make them less overwhelming over time.

Our emotions have important functions and the more we understand their roles and what they are trying to do, the better we can manage them. First, let's talk about the universal emotions. These include happiness, sadness, fear, disgust, shame, and surprise. These six emotions are believed to be expressed similarly (i.e., using the same gestures and facial expressions) everywhere in the world. They're almost like primary colors – acting as basic emotions that can also combine together to form others. For example, jealousy, such as that which Draco often feels toward Harry, is a combination of a few different emotions such as fear (of not being as good as Harry), anger (at Harry for taking away his spotlight), and disgust (with Harry and his friends). Emotions, like paint colors, can also vary in intensity – sometimes we might feel sad, as someone might feel about losing a Quiddich match, at other times we might feel depressed or devastated, like what Harry feels after Sirius' death.

According to psychologist Patty Resick, PhD who specializes in treating people with posttraumatic stress disorder (PTSD), we have two types of emotional responses after a specific event – *natural* (or situation-based) and *manufactured* (or interpretation-based). For example, when Harry is involuntarily selected to participate in the Triwizard Tournament, he is anxious and confused. These are natural emotions to occur based on the events. On the other hand, Ron believes that Harry somehow cheated in order to be selected and feels jealous and angry. His emotions are based on his interpretations rather than on the event itself. Natural emotions tend to fade over time, provided that we allow ourselves to experience and process them. On the other hand, manufactured emotions are likely to linger because they are stuck to our (often incorrect) interpretation of the situation.

Emotions can also be affected by situations, which remind us of our past experiences. For example, the mere mention of Dolores Umbridge, might be enough to make Harry feel angry, remembering how cruel she'd been to him. In addition, the mention of her name might even cause some physiological changes in his body, possibly causing his heart to beat faster. He might feel a surge of adrenaline, as well as tension in his shoulders, and a tightening of his fists. He might even feel a twinge of pain on the back of his hand (right hand in the book, left hand in the movie), where Umbridge's enchanted quill pierced his skin like a scalpel as a form of punishment.

It is not uncommon to feel a change of emotions and physiological sensations when we are reminded of a specific event. Our bodies sometimes react to a mere memory of an event as if it is happening right now. Our body can also do that if we imagine how an event might play out in the future. For example, when Hermione imagines failing her O.W.L. exams, her body is likely reacting with the same amount of distress as if she were to actually fail them.

Although they are sometimes uncomfortable, our emotions and our physiology can be very helpful in that they can, for example, prepare us for danger. When Harry and his friends break into the Ministry of Magic believing that the Death Eaters had captured Sirius, they are understandably feeling scared and anxious. These emotions are actually helpful to them in that moment in terms of ensuring that they are ready to protect themselves from danger. When we are in danger, our adrenaline response (also known as *fight-flight-or-freeze* response) is the very superpower, the very *Protego Totalum* spell that we need. Our adrenaline response allows us to think faster, move faster, and be stronger in order to survive whatever threat, whatever Death Eater we are faced with. Adrenaline allows our hearts to beat faster, pumping more blood to our vital organs. It allows us to breathe faster, getting more oxygen into our lungs. We might feel jittery; it is because the adrenaline in our bodies is trying to make us move to confront our enemy and to avoid danger. This adrenaline also gives us more speed and more strength than we might normally have. When we feel most anxious, most afraid, is when we are strongest.

The fight-flight-or-freeze response does not only show up when we are actually in danger. It also shows up in situations, which *remind* us of danger, sometimes causing false alarms in our bodies. For example, although boggarts, the shape-shifting non-beings, which take the shape of whatever we are most afraid of, are not actually dangerous, we might be scared of them. Harry, who was understandably afraid of the Dementors, was similarly affected by the boggarts, even though the boggarts could not actually harm him. Remaining in a situation that makes us uncomfortable long enough to recognize which threat is real and which isn't can allow us to reduce false alarms, and reduce anxiety and other adrenaline responses that come with them.

Although emotions can be caused by an event or by a thought, sometimes they can also occur "out of nowhere." Just like weather changes, our emotions change as well. In exploring emotions with my ten year old son, I've taught him to be able to say, "I feel sad because I am sad." This holds true for me, as well as millions of others who sometimes might feel depressed, irritable, angry, or anxious for no apparent reason. We do not need to always have a reason for why we feel a certain way. We just do. Instead of trying to control and predict our emotions, we can allow ourselves to experience the emotions that show up.

Whichever emotion you are feeling, no matter how uncomfortable it is, remember, emotions are not your enemy. Emotions are informative. Even if there is no obvious cause for them, they might indicate something that you might need. Our emotional needs might include physical or emotional safety, the need for love, attention, validation, assurance, support, or rest. Reflecting on what we might need might allow us to be better able to soothe ourselves in that moment.

In fact, there are research studies, which suggest that all emotions including depression have a very important function – they remind us that we might need some time to heal and gather our resources. When Professor Lockhart's fails at healing an injury Harry suffers, it results in the boy losing all the bones in one of his arms and he has to spend the night in the hospital wing, waiting for them to regrow. Similarly, when we experience an emotional injury, recent or even a distant one, we might sometimes need to give ourselves permission to heal, to gather our strength and resources. People who are able to allow such rest and self-care for themselves are more likely to recover faster than those who attempt to "push-through" the physical and emotional pain.

Let's explore some of the most common emotions that nearly all witches and wizards feel at one point or another. In the table below there are four columns. The column on the left lists some common emotions. The next two columns list examples of *Harry Potter* characters that experienced these emotions, as well as the functions of these emotions. See if you can fill out the column on the right with examples of your own experiences with these emotions.

Emotion	Examples	Function	Your experiences
Angry	Ron when Draco bullies Hermione	To protect ourselves or others	
Ashamed	Lupin, of being werewolf; Sirius, of his family; Dursleys of Harry	To try to fit in, to avoid being judged or rejected; need soothing/ connection	
Depressed	Anyone exposed to Dementors; Harry after Dumbledore dies	To try to heal from the painful emotional experience; need support	
Disgusted	Harry is disgusted with Dudley & Aunt Marge	To avoid toxicity, including toxic food or people	
Embarrassed	Ron when he receives howler	To try to fit in, to avoid that behavior in the future	
Empathic	Luna explaining to Harry about the Thestrals	To connect with and help others	
Excited	Harry learning to fly; Hermione before Hogwarts	To feel joy in meaningful experiences	
Frustrated	Snape trying to teach Harry Legilimency	To expel energy when things are not going the way we'd like	
Guilty	Ron for hurting Hermione's feelings in their first year	To change unhelpful behavior in the future	
Happy	When Harry is at Hogwarts; when Harry sees or remembers his parents	To experience joy, to promote engagement in activities and connections we care about	

Emotion	Examples	Function	Your experiences
Hateful	Harry hates Voldemort; Petunia hates Harry; Snape hates James	Comes from pain, functions to protect ourselves from further pain	
Hopeful	Fred & George when leaving Hogwarts to start business	To motivate change	
Irritable	Harry after Cedric's death; Harry when trying to figure out the Triwizard task	To signal us that we might need a break/support	
Jealous	Ron is often jealous of Harry and his brothers	To look for reassurance & emotional safety	
Overwhelmed	Harry when he is not sure where to find the Horcruxes	To signal us that we might need guidance	
Panicked	Wormtail about getting caught; Hermione about exams	To get us to safety; to enable action (studying for exams, for example)	
Scared	Ron is scared of spiders	To seek safety away from the threat	
Surprised	Harry when he learns he is a wizard	To evaluate the new information	
Vulnerable	Harry when he asks out Cho Chang; Hermione when she confronts Ron at Yule Ball	To connect with people or experiences that are most meaningful	

I hope that you are able to see that emotions are acceptable and all are okay to experience. Our emotions are not our actions. Our emotions just are. Most of them arise out of our desire to belong, to connect with something or someone. While it might be scary and uncomfortable to experience these emotions, they are all an essential part of what makes us magical. All of these can be quite vulnerable to experience and magic usually happens right outside of our comfort zone. If we step out of our comfort zone, we are more likely to find magic than if we stay in it.

Here are some examples of times when we might feel vulnerable, anxious, and scared and where the magic can truly happen:

- When we say "I love you" first
- When we apologize or ask for forgiveness
- When we reach out to ask for help
- When we offer help
- When we try to see another person's point of view even if we don't agree with them

Charms Homework: Name and observe your emotions for at least a few minutes every day. See if you can start identifying their functions and what you might need to do to support yourself as you experience them. Greet them as a friend, and see if you can get to know them.

CHAPTER 6

SELF-COMPASSION TRANSFIGURATION

"Words are, in my not-so-humble opinion, our most inexhaustible source of magic. Capable of both inflicting injury, and remedying it."

- ALBUS DUMBLEDORE, *HARRY POTTER AND THE DEATHLY HALLOWS*

DURING HIS TIME as a Hogwarts student, Severus Snape is viciously bullied by Harry's father, James, and his friends, who are collectively called *The Marauders*. At one point, the Marauders levitate Snape and embarrass him in front of the entire school by flashing his underpants.

Snape, who excels at Defense Against the Dark Arts and Potions, develops a number of spells and potions while still a student. One of the curses he develops, *Sectumsempra,* is especially designed to be used on enemies. It's name translates from Latin to mean "to cut forever" and the curse lives up to its name. It cuts deep, gushing blood, continuously injuring the victim until someone performs its counter spell, *Vulnera Sanentur*, ("to heal the wound").

The metaphoric representation of *Sectumsempra* can be found in our everyday lives. Has anyone ever said something extremely painful to you, something which hurt you a long time after those words were said?

It is hard enough to be exposed to the *Sectumsempra* curses coming from others, but we also often inflict them upon ourselves through *self-bullying*. Self-bullying involves shaming and putting ourselves down, and emotionally or physically hurting ourselves, as Dobby, the house elf often does. Have you ever shamed yourself for making a mistake, for not doing a perfect job at something, having you ever called yourself "an idiot," or shamed yourself, based on your appearance, performance, or ability? These are all examples of self-bullying. Chances are you would never say those things to others, and chances are that you would be highly unlikely to use such *Sectumsempra* curse on others. Yet, we use it on ourselves.

Have you ever heard the famous Muggle expression, "sticks and stones will break my bones but words can never hurt me?" Not only is this expression misleading in terms of emotional pain, but as it turns out, verbal teasing, taunting, and bullying can negatively affect our physiology similarly to physical abuse. There are specific areas in our brain that are responsible for pain perception (for example, the anterior cingulate cortex). These same brain regions are also active when we are experiencing emotional abuse, witness someone we care about being abused, or when we are remembering a physically or emotionally painful experience. This means that our pain, whether physical or emotional, is in fact real, both affecting the pain receptors in our brain, in the same way.

> *"Of course it is happening inside your head, Harry, but why on earth should that mean that it is not real?"*
>
> - Albus Dumbledore, *Harry Potter and the Deathly Hallows*

In the late 1990's, researchers at Kaiser Permanente Hospital in San Diego, California collected data from over 9,500 participants creating one of the largest and most comprehensive data analyses about the participants' physical and emotional health. The data focused on the effects of participants' adverse childhood events (ACEs) on their health. ACEs included physical abuse, emotional abuse, sexual assault, death of a parent, household dysfunction, family history of imprisonment, and others. The results of the study found that people with four or more ACEs were much more likely to experience depression, anxiety, substance abuse, or attempt self-harm or suicide. These individuals were also much more likely to develop heart disease, liver disease, lung disease, or sexually transmitted diseases (STDs), and die at an earlier age.

In addition, people with a history of ACEs are more likely to experience physical pain, more prone to developing PTSD, are more likely to be easily overwhelmed and anxious, more likely to experience chronic headaches and stomach aches, irritable bowel syndrome (IBS), and potentially produce changes in their DNA.

These findings would imply that people like Harry, who experience significant maltreatment in early childhood, are at higher risk of being affected by the Dementors of depression and the boggarts of anxiety, as well as more likely to be affected by tragic losses and traumatic experiences, compared to people without such history. That is, in fact, what we see in the books. The effects that the Dementors have on Harry seem much stronger compared to his best friends, Ron and Hermione, who undoubtedly had fewer ACEs growing up. This is not to say that their experiences with Dementors are not real. They are. Rather, what it means is that Harry has a greater risk of being negatively affected by them.

What Harry truly needs after all his struggles is for someone to be compassionate and understanding. People like Professor Dumbledore, Mrs. Weasley, and Professor Lupin provide Harry with the compassion and support that he needs when they are with him. The necessity of other people's compassion in Harry's life is (in my opinion) unquestionable. And chances are that when we see other people in our lives who are going through a hard time, we probably support them in some way. Clearly, some physically and emotionally painful events can be detrimental to our health, and what most of us need in those moments is understanding and support. Why then is it so challenging for us to extend that same level of love and compassion toward ourselves when we are going through a hard time?

There are several reasons why people might struggle with self-compassion. For example, some people might believe that self-bullying is necessary in motivating themselves. Alternatively, some might believe that if they practice self-compassion, they are being selfish or overindulgent.

Let's take a closer look at each of these reasons. Many people find that they use self-bullying to motivate themselves: *Stop being lazy, you idiot! Other people have it so much worse than you! You are such a loser! If other people found out the truth about you, they would reject you.*

In the short-term self-bullying might actually get us moving. We might start a stringent new diet, a bullet-proof exercise plan, or a competitive new project. In the long-term, however, we are bound to have a setback, whether it's through eating a pumpkin pasty or a toffee treacle when we are trying to maintain a gluten-free, dairy-free, sugar-free raw diet, or whether it's missing a few days, or weeks or months of Quidditch exercise. It is here, in this setback, that our decisions matter most. We can shame ourselves, so much so that we give up altogether, or we can use *self-compassion*. Self-compassion refers to treating ourselves with the same care and kindness that we would use with our loved ones, or our favorite fictional characters if we met them in real life.

The second misconception about self-compassion is the belief that self-compassion means overindulgence. In reality, these are opposite concepts. Whereas indulgence implies excessive over-gratification, self-compassion refers to giving ourselves the support that we need in order to get back to doing what is important to us. Hence, drinking a six-pack of butterbeers just because you've had a rough day is not self-compassion, but rather, a form of overindulgence. Self-compassion would mean using a kind, supportive voice when we notice that we are struggling to remind us that we are not alone and to remind us what is really important to us. So, when we have broken our extremely stringent diet, rather than torturing ourselves in a way that would make Umbridge seem like our guardian angel, we can instead implement Dumbledore's wisdom. Dumbledore would inevitably mention that we all indulge sometimes, we all get into trouble and have setbacks. And, at the same time, we can always choose to get back to what is truly important to us, whether it is our health, our fandom, our education, or our career. In fact, research studies show that people who practice self-compassion in this way are more likely to maintain their motivation in the face on a setback than those who are judging themselves. When Harry is first learning to face the Dementor-shaped boggarts, he is unsuccessful at summoning the protective Patronus charm. He is visibly frustrated with this, but through Professor Lupin's patience and compassion, Harry allows himself to continue and is eventually successful at producing this advanced spell. On the other hand, when Harry is learning Occlumency, a spell intended to block out Voldemort's ability to read and influence Harry's mind, he is also struggling. However, Professor Snape, who is tutoring Harry in Occlumency, is highly impatient and critical of Harry. For this and other reasons, Harry does not quite get the hang of Occlumency practice until the end of his 7th year in the series.

It seems that as we practice self-compassion, we are more likely to be persistent with our goals and are more likely to feel better physically and emotionally. In fact, barring emergency situations, it is usually important to practice compassion toward ourselves first before we take care of other people or other responsibilities. This might strike some people as "selfish"(Third misconception about self-compassion). However, in a lot of ways, engaging in self-compassion is not only the wisest, it is also the kindest, and the most compassionate thing we can do for others. When we are taking care of everything and everyone else, we are likely to burn out, to become physically and mentally exhausted and might therefore struggle with helping. Self-compassion, in this case, is an investment in the fuel of our self-care so that we have the strength and the energy to take care of others. If you've ever flown on an airplane, you've probably heard the flight attendants announce that in case of a drop in cabin pressure, oxygen masks will be available for passengers. The passengers are instructed to put on *their own* masks first *before* assisting others. Why is that? This is done to ensure that we are able to maintain consciousness in order to help the people around us, otherwise, we might not be able to help others in the most crucial moments. Self-compassion, therefore, is any intentional act of self-kindness, recharge, and healing toward ourselves, which allows us then to return to engaging in the activities that matter most to us, and can allow us to accept, rather than shame, ourselves.

For example, Kiki reported that self-acceptance through the *Harry Potter* fandom helped her overcome a history of abuse and learn to better manage her mental health struggles.

Kiki's story

My love of Harry Potter started in a classroom when I was nine but I didn't see the magic until I was around twelve years old. What I learnt through Harry Potter couldn't be taught by the words I was reading but by feeling what the characters did. I connected with Harry first, I had a very real kinship with the boy who hated the summer where he was forced to stay indoors with his oppressive guardians. I didn't realize it then but the franchise was helping me stave off not only boredom during my summer confinement but the beginnings of my long arduous journey with mental disorders.

I was angry a lot for most of my adolescence and by nineteen, I had lost my first love to addiction. I had been abusing my body with self-injury, yet threw in drug and alcohol abuse and self-neglect like fuel onto an already out of control fire. Throughout these points in my life I have always used Harry Potter as a means of escape, as entertainment but mainly as a source of material designed to make me feel less alone in the world. The connection to the characters felt personal, these people were just like me and if they could survive, then so could I.

It was in my early twenties where I started claiming the quiet confidence of one Remus Lupin - society had condemned my visible wounds and rejected me but Hogwarts and its residents welcomed me home. As the battle with my mental health raged on inside of me, I sought comfort within the walls of the castle. I found self-acceptance, I understood that my mental disorders were not going to go away and it offered me a unique position of being a safe space for other people during trying times.

The franchise was compromised when I entered into what became a 2-and-a-half-year relationship that was emotionally, sexually and financially abusive. I lost faith and hope in the one place that in almost two decades, had never failed me. Times can be almost irrevocably dark, my judgment gets clouded and I become a fixture in Azkaban, rooted to the spot in fear, with a swarm of Dementors blanketing my every waking hour.

Everything I have learnt, everything I have discovered had been sucked straight out of my soul and it leaves me broken and hollow. It was here that I eventually found I was able to stay strong under the pressures of the world - from the abuse, victim blaming to self-shaming - and to hold fast to what I know to be right. My Patronus became my truth, a newly revived sense of self, a brilliant beacon of light that overcomes the darkness and allows me to see my abuser for what he truly was. It is the strength I have obtained to devote my art and my craft to creating an awareness of mental health and abuse through poetry and storytelling. It allows me to show people that they are not alone and together we can smash down the barriers that make talking about mental health socially taboo.

Like Kiki, I've struggled with moderate-severe depression and feelings of worthlessness most of my life. One of my biggest struggles entailed my self-shaming about my appearance. Specifically, I always judged myself for being "not skinny enough" and for my stomach being "not flat enough." There were many occasions where I would cancel plans with my friends because I was too ashamed to have them see me "looking so fat and ugly." I would never have judged anyone else for how they look, but when it came to me, I was never good enough. There were days that I would punch myself in the stomach, hard, saying "I hate you." What I failed to notice was that the more I hated my stomach, the more it hurt; and the more it hurt, the more I hated it, feeling depressed and ashamed of my *imperfect* appearance.

Then, a few years ago I began learning about self-compassion. In one of the self-compassion courses I took, the instructor asked us to close our eyes and consider what we shame ourselves about the most. It was easy. My attention immediately went to my gut, wanting to suck it in, holding my breath, feeling myself fill up with self-loathing and self-disgust. Then, the instructor asked us to notice *where* in our body we experienced most of our shame.

Well, wouldn't you know it? I felt all my shame in my gut. In fact, I learned that the stomach is the place where most our emotions are formed and experienced, allowing us to process guilt and shame, as well as excitement, fear, and anxiety. It is where our intuition lives, our "gut feeling," our biggest and most important source of magic. And when we sense danger, when we are hurt, or when we are hurting ourselves, the blood vessels in our stomach constrict, creating an effect which for some people feels like hunger, for others feels like nausea or stomach ache, causing some to have the need to release their bowels (triggering IBS), triggering a potential migraine response in some people, and triggering depression or anxiety in others by affecting the adrenal glands or suppressing the production of serotonin, one of the body's "feel good chemicals." In short, what this means is that the very area I was so blatantly abusing, is the one that needs love, support, and compassion the most. And when we abuse it, we essentially hurt ourselves even more than we are already hurting.

During my exercise, the instructor then told us to imagine our stomach, chest, or any other part of our body where we feel shame, as a little child, as someone separate from us, (perhaps someone like little Harry Potter, or little Luna Lovegood, or little Severus Snape) at a time when they needed love, support, and reassurance the most. We then had to cradle the part of our body where we felt shame and treat it with kindness for a brief period of time. This exercise was both excruciating and also extremely freeing. For the first time in my life I saw my stomach not as an enemy, not as something ugly about myself that I, like Aunt Petunia, needed to hide away, but rather as something that was worthy of love and compassion, just like a little child, or a little puppy or kitten.

When I first met my husband, he confided in me how ashamed he was of the size of his stomach and punched himself in the gut in front of me. I softly took his hands away and kissed his stomach. I told him that his stomach is one of the most beautiful things about him, and that it is the area that needs the most love and compassion. He now does the same for me. I still have days when I become self-conscious about how I look but I no longer hit myself and neither does my partner.

Self-compassion practice does not only help us feel better about ourselves, it can also help us improve our physical and mental health. When mammals are struggling, they require some form of nurturance, whether it's through an embrace, reassurance, or physical warmth. Receiving kindness from others, as well as from ourselves can turn the stress-based *fight-flight-or-freeze response* into a calming *rest-and-digest* response. In addition, when we are receiving nurturance, our bodies release *oxytocin,* a "feel-good" or "cuddle" hormone (the ultimate Patronus charm) which can soothe us in the moment of suffering.

Interestingly, these beneficial effects can also occur when we are supporting someone else who is struggling. In fact, some research findings suggest that people who help others are less likely to die from stress compared to those who do not, implying that helping and connecting with others might prolong lifespan, and maybe make us more resilient when it comes to facing our own real-life Death Eater stressors.

Since self-compassion seems to be such a crucial part of Defense Against the Dark Arts, let us identify its elements and determine some ways that we can practice it. Self-compassion consists of three basic elements – mindfulness (see Chapter 3), as well as common humanity, and self-kindness.

MINDFULNESS – THE ESSENCE OF DITTANY

The first element of self-compassion is mindfulness – the ability to notice that we are struggling and that we might need support. The exact way this plays out might vary from person to person. For some people, the mindfulness element of self-compassion might be noticing the increase in their anxiety or depression. For others it might be noticing that they are starting to become overwhelmed, irritable, or experiencing a start or an increase in physical pain.

For some of us, certain stresses and situations, such as being in a crowded place, hearing a loud repeating sound, having too much to do and too little time to do it in, or having to interact with a lot of people might be exhausting. The overwhelm we might feel in some of these situations is almost like being splinched while apparating – it might make us feel as if we are being torn to pieces. Mindfulness can function like the healing Essence of Dittany potion in this case. For example, when we are overwhelmed, we can observe this emotion, see how it is manifesting, and take a few breaths or stretches to allow ourselves to better cope with the situation.

THE LEGILIMENCY SPELL: COMMON HUMANITY

> *"We are all human, aren't we? Every human life is worth the same, and worth saving."*
>
> –KINGSLEY SHACKLEBOLT, *HARRY POTTER AND THE DEATHLY HALLOWS*

The second element of self-compassion is *common humanity,* which means recognizing that we are not alone in our experiences. Although logically, we might realize that millions of other people might have struggled with at least some of the same experiences as we do, it is hard to remember that fact during our actual struggle. It is hard enough to experience depression, anxiety, insecurity, the desire to self-harm, or addiction. It is much harder to go through it if we are shaming ourselves and therefore alienating ourselves from others, or hiding out.

On the other hand, when we realize that we are not alone in our struggles and that many, many people might be experiencing very similar things that we are in that very moment, it can make this experience more bearable. In addition, sharing our experiences with others who can understand them, or those who have been through something similar, can help us feel less alone, and can help us begin our healing journey.

I imagine that, like me, many of you while reading the *Harry Potter* series found yourselves in at least some aspects of some of the characters. Some of you might value learning or have anxiety like Hermione. Some of you might have been bullied like Snape was, or experienced a loss or abuse when you were younger, just like Snape and Harry. For many of us these books are potentially healing because they connect us with aspects of ourselves we might otherwise be unable to understand. These books remind us that perhaps *just like Harry,* we too want to find a sense of belonging, or perhaps *just like Luna,* some of us do not always fit in, or perhaps *just like Lupin* we might have a side of ourselves we feel uncomfortable sharing with others. Yet, connecting with these books and characters within, we might be able to find ourselves.

For example, Amanda shares her experience of connection with the *Harry Potter* fandom and what it has meant to her.

Amanda's story

I was already thirty years of age when my older sister finally convinced me to read Harry Potter. We were on a family vacation. I had two small children at the time. Everyday after lunch and swimming, my kids went down for a nap and it became Harry Potter reading hour.

Immediately, the series sparked a creative chord in me. After reading Chapter 6 "The Journey to Platform Nine and Three Quarters," I couldn't wait to have some sort of party and make up all the treats that the Trolley witch had sold on the Hogwarts Express train. My first creative endeavor; I made my own chocolate frogs in clear bags with hand lettered header labels and Harry Potter stickers inside. These were made and handed out to any Harry Potter reader I knew, every time a new book, or movie was released.

This time period was the beginning of my time as a full time at-home mom. During this time, I had learned that I had depression. Harry Potter was the only thing that I felt defined me as myself, not just as a wife or a mother. It was my escape, my pleasure, my time for myself.

When my two kids got a little older, we began to read the books together at bedtime. When Harry Potter themed toys came out, I was more than happy to get them for my kids. It helped me connect with my children as we found Harry Potter things to do together, build Harry Potter Lego sets, make up HP songs, movies, scrapbooks, dress-ups, Backyard Quidditch, make Hogwarts school books and candy potions for their Harry and Hermione dolls, just to name a few.

After reading the fifth book unconscionably quick, I was so eager to have my questions answered, I started theorizing what I thought should happen, or wanted to happen, that I began to write my first fan fiction. I had so much fun doing that, I ended up writing three more!

When the public hype from the seven books and eight movies were over, I began to get depressed about it. One day, by accident, I found out there was a Harry Potter Meet-Up group in my area. This is what I needed. The friends I had, that read the books with me, had moved on to other things. I needed to meet new people who were still into Harry Potter and wanted to keep the magic alive as much as I did. Normally, I am very shy and would not want to meet a bunch of random strangers by myself, but for Harry Potter, I would forgo my introvertedness and seek out my road to happiness.

Harry Potter helps me stay active, inspires me to be creative, and helps me to connect with other people. If Patronuses were real, mine would be the shape of Harry Potter because I am the most happy when I am involved in that world. It inspires me to be the best version of me I can be. It is the chocolate to my Dementors!

In connections with others, we might be able to find healing just like Amanda did. And through connections with real people or even fictional characters, we might be able to develop our sense of empathy. It is almost as if we were practicing the Legilimency spell, a spell that allows us to see inside the minds of others. Legilimency allows us to have empathy toward other people, having a better understanding about where they are coming from. As much as Harry hates Snape, when he learns about Snape's history of being abused as a child and being bullied as a Hogwarts student, he identifies with him and feels for him.

When we empathize with others, the way that Harry does with Snape or the way that Queenie Goldstein from *Fantastic Beasts and Where to Find Them* does with Jacob, we might recognize that these individuals deserve to be treated with kindness and do not deserve to experience abuse and pain. In fact, when Harry learns that his own father and his friends tortured Snape, he is angry with them, feeling empathy toward Snape.

Just as understanding others allows us to experience empathy toward them, so can an understanding of ourselves. It stands to reason that if other people, or even fictional characters, deserve our empathy, then so do we. Just like Harry, we also deserve love and protection. Just like Ron, we also deserve to know that we are loved and wanted, and just like Hermione, we deserve to be appreciated for all our efforts.

Furthermore, sometimes having empathy for ourselves and others can help us better understand why some people might have hurt us. *"Hurt people hurt people,"* a famous saying goes. This means that those who are hurting others usually do so because they themselves have been hurt. Characters like Snape and Petunia, both of whom made Harry's lives miserable due to their dislike of his parents, demonstrate how much a person's own pain can dictate their abusive actions toward others. We should never have to put up with abuse. However, sometimes understanding and having compassion for both ourselves and the person who might be hurting us, might, at least in some situations, help us better understand and hopefully, process the situation in a safe way.

EXPECTO PATRONUM! A SELF-KINDNESS PRACTICE

In triaging any situation, the person who is hurt the most should be the one who receives most immediate care. That includes you. When we are struggling, we need to offer kindness to ourselves (i.e., *self-kindness*) in order to allow ourselves to soothe, heal, and gain more physical and emotional strength.

Self-kindness can be a big action, such as taking a vacation or getting a massage. Alternatively, self-compassion can be a small action, such as wrapping yourself up in a blanket (perhaps one with your House symbol on it), or drinking hot chocolate or pumpkin juice, taking a few breaths, or giving yourself a soothing hug by placing the palms of your hands on your heart center. Other examples include engaging with our fandom, using an ice pack or a heating pad (especially in case of physical pain), lying down, reading a book, or watching a funny clip in order help us better cope with our physical or emotional pain. These smaller self-compassion practices are sometimes called "self-compassion on the go" since they can be done nearly anytime.

These self-compassion practices might not *take away* our suffering but they might help us better manage our struggle. For example, when Hermione cries over having to modify her parents' memories, Ron puts his arm around her. This action will not reverse what happened, nor will it take away Hermione's pain. However, he puts his arm around her to comfort her, to support her. Similarly, we can give ourselves small (or large) tokens of support, not to take away our pain (which is often not possible), but merely because we are a human being who is struggling and who deserves love and support.

Another way of practicing self-kindness is through kind language, kind phrasing, or writing. For example, if you were to write a compassionate and encouraging letter to the ten year old Harry when he was still living in the cupboard under the stairs at the Dursleys' house, what would you write? What kind of words of wisdom and support would you want to convey? What would you specifically want him to understand?

What about a letter to Neville when Snape is picking on him, or perhaps a letter to Hermione when she is crying in the bathroom after Ron insulted her in their first year at Hogwarts?

Now imagine for a moment that you were writing a letter to you, perhaps a younger you, back then, back in the time when perhaps you were little and scared and just needed to know that every thing would be okay. What would you want to say to yourself? What would you want to remind yourself of?

Now, imagine for a moment that you are talking to Dumbledore, a mentor, someone who is full of wisdom and compassion. What would he say to you? What kind of wisdom would he give you, what words of wisdom would he share?

For some people the kind phrases they long to hear from others might include a wish, such as:

May you be happy.
May you be safe.
May you know how loved you are.
May you feel your magical potential.
May you know how much you matter.

These phrases are called *Loving Kindness Meditation*. Feel free to adjust these phrases or come up with your own phrases, hopefully ones which make you feel supported, safe, and maybe even grateful. See if you can notice the effects of these practices on yourself and others.

Tranfiguration practice: This week, see if you can practice with small self-kindness gestures for yourself ("self-compassion on the go") and try out the Loving Kindness Kindness Meditation. You can find and listen to guided Loving Kindness Meditation practices or you can try it silently on your own.

CHAPTER 7

THE DEFUSION INCANTATION

"What you fear most of all is – fear. Very wise."

– Remus Lupin, *Harry Potter and The Prisoner of Azkaban*

During their third year at Hogwarts, Harry and Ron enroll in a Divination class taught by Professor Sybil Trelawney. The very first time she meets Harry, Trelawney sees the mark of a Grim in his teacup and responds in horror that this mark means his untimely death. This, of course, terrifies Harry, whose life has already been threatened three times by Lord Voldemort at this point. Over the course of his time at Hogwarts, Harry witnesses Trelawney make hundreds of terrifying predictions, most of them never coming true. In fact, in her entire life, of all the predictions she had made, only two of Trelawney's prophecies actually come true. That's two out of (approximately) 50,000 predictions.*

---

* This is assuming that Trelawney makes at least five predictions per day for at least thirty years.

If she were a psychic in your local neighborhood psychic shop and had a 2/50,000 chance of being right, you probably would not trust anything she predicts.

Our minds sometimes work kind of like Professor Trelawney's predictions. We too might take certain signs in our environment to predict danger when they might not. For example, when we are unable to reach a loved one, some of us might think that they might have died in a terrible accident or imagine other worst case scenarios. We might also believe that our friends are angry with us if we do not get a reply to our text messages, possibly reviewing our previous conversations in great detail to see where we went wrong.

In moments of anxiety, it can feel as if our worries were hit with an Engorgio Charm, making the probabilities of a catastrophe seem bigger than they really are. This process is called *catastrophizing* and most of us engage in it at one point or another. People who struggle with anxiety are more likely to engage in frequent catastrophizing. Current statistics indicate that at least 18% of adults in the United States struggle with *diagnosed* anxiety, and estimate that approximately 30% struggle with anxiety overall. If these statistics are accurate, this means that one in every three people you know struggles with anxiety and probably experiences frequent catastrophizing.

Our thoughts can actually influence our feelings and our behaviors. Similarly, our behaviors can affect our thoughts and feelings. The following diagram shows the two-directional relationship of each of these components: Thoughts, Feelings, and Behaviors. All affect one another.

THOUGHTS

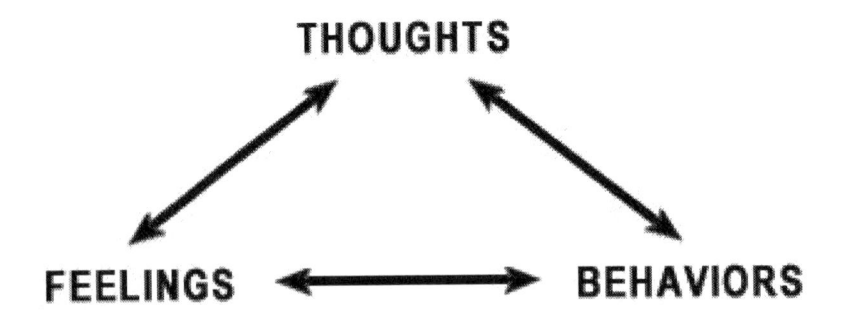

FEELINGS ⟷ **BEHAVIORS**

For example, someone like Neville, who might have a thought that he is going to embarrass himself in front of Professor Snape, is likely to feel very anxious when he has to do magic in front of Snape, and therefore is likely to try to avoid brewing potions in front of him. Neville's thoughts, in this case, might be affecting his emotions, as well as his behaviors. Similarly, in avoiding making potions in front of Snape, Neville reinforces the belief that he is "incapable." Therefore, he is more likely to feel anxious if he has to do magic in Snape's classroom in the future.

Since these components – thoughts, feelings, and behaviors, are all connected and affect one another, we need to break this interconnected cycle in order to reduce the impact of certain thoughts and emotions on our lives. We already talked about using mindfulness (Chapter 3) and self compassion (Chapter 6) to help us better manage our difficult emotions. We can also work on reducing catastrophizing ("*Engorgio*") and other uncomfortable thoughts that might hold us back by applying Reducio (Shrinking Charm). In this case, Reducio involves taking the power away from the thought by acknowledging the thought for what it is – a thought, as opposed to a fact. Often, we *fuse* with our thoughts, habitually taking them at face value. Thoughts such as, *"I'm a failure"* or *"everyone is judging me"* are both examples of thoughts we might fuse with, potentially leading o these thoughts controlling how we feel and what we do.

In order to combat fusion, we can try a *defusion incantation.* For example, instead of saying/thinking, *"I'm a failure"* or *"everyone is judging me,"* we can instead say, *"I am having the thought that I am a failure"* or *"I am having the thought that everyone is judging me."* By taking this objective, Moody's eye-like, examining approach, we can take away some of the power from the thought, noticing that in some ways, it is no more valid than the thought *"I'm a banana tree."*

If we were to read an article in papers and tablous such as *The Daily Prophet* or *The Quibbler*, we probably wouldn't just blindly believe everything we read, but rather note that a news story is sometimes true and sometimes isn't. We can treat our thoughts in the same manner.

Give it a try. See if you can verbally state your thoughts out loud for one minute and see if there is a difference in the impact these thoughts have on you. They might not take away your emotions, but hopefully, this defusion practice takes away some of the control these thought have on you.

CHECK-IN.

How did it go? Most people notice that over time the thoughts become less impactful and less overwhelming.

Another way to practice defusion is to incorporate mindfulness and compassion toward our thoughts and emotions. Imagine if you could have tea (or coffee, if you prefer) with your thoughts and your feelings, what would they look like? I'm imagining mine as Fang, Hagrid's dog. Sure, he is big and scary in his appearance, but once you get to know him, you might realize that he is actually scared of everything and therefore his actions might be driven by fear. What if you could then comfort Fang? Or even Fluffy, the enormous three-headed-dog, guarding the entrance to the passageway to the Philosopher's Stone. What if you realized that the very thoughts and emotions you were so afraid of were actually themselves driven by fear and in their misguided, Dobby-like desire to protect you, actually lead you to experience pain and discomfort. Dobby is a house elf, who tries very hard to protect Harry from danger. Unfortunately, Dobby's very attempts at protecting Harry often lead to him getting injured.

If we can find some compassion and understanding for our thoughts and emotions, perhaps we not only can reduce their impact on us but also respond to them. For example, when having a thought, such as, *"everyone is judging me,"* perhaps we can thank your mind (or our inner Dobby) for looking out for us, but continue our journey anyway.

> *"It is the unknown we fear when we look upon death and darkness, nothing more."*
>
> – ALBUS DUMBLEDORE, *HARRY POTTER AND THE HALF-BLOOD PRINCE*

When terrible things happen to us or around us, we might feel afraid that they will continue happening. For example, after numerous losses, Harry did not want his friends or any members of the Order of Phoenix to accompany him in his search for Horcruxes. Similarly, after terrible accidents or terrorist attacks, we might be frightened to travel and attend certain places, or wish to avoid certain activities. To face our fears, be it our thoughts or emotions, is to use the Expelliarmus spell on our enemy, as Cassie describes in her story below. The more we examine and get to know our fears, the less frightening they might become. The more we get to know our fears, the less frightening they might become.

Cassie's Story

Nearly 3,000 people lost their lives. Families lost brothers, sisters, mothers, daughters, husbands and wives. I, like most people alive on September 11, 2001 remember everything about that day vividly. I was in the seventh grade, and I was eating breakfast in the living room before school, when my Dad came in and turned on the television and told me to watch. As I watched replay after replay of the first plane crash into the first of the Twin Towers, I didn't understand what was happening. It seemed like a terrible and tragic accident. While I sat there finishing breakfast, some twenty minutes or so later, there was the second plane crashing into the one tower still standing. Still, as a twelve year old child I could not understand the ramifications of what was happening. It is really difficult to explain the concept of terrorism to a child, and the motives behind such barbarism and hate. As young kids, some of us children of the Harry Potter Generation, tried to hang on to our innocence, much like Harry when he was thrust into the magical world at the age of eleven, but instead we lived every day in fear that terrorists would attack once again and that we might lose our parents. Harry Potter gave us a world to escape into, and some means to understand what was happening to us. Harry Potter represents the youth of America in that he was innocent, and didn't know what was coming his way. He became the poster-boy for our generation, and the hero that pulled us out of dark times because we believed that for the time we were reading that magic was real. We believed that even the most unlikely people, kids even, can be a hero in someone's eyes.

I was eleven when I embarked on my Harry Potter journey, and I desperately awaited an owl to bring my acceptance letter to Hogwarts, and while it may have never came in the physical form, today I feel like a proud Hogwarts graduate.

MAKING OUR BOGGARTS LOOK RIDDIKULUS

In Harry's 3rd year at Hogwarts, Professor Lupin teaches his students how to manage their fears in the best way possible – by facing them (instead of running away from them) and making them seem ridiculous. He makes them practice on creatures called Boggarts. The Boggarts take the shape of the very object, person, or situation that most terrifies the person near it.

Other than Harry, the student who arguably benefits most from this lesson is Neville Longbottom. Neville, who has been bullied, shamed, and terrorized by Professor Snape, is unsurprisingly afraid of him. When he sees the Snape-looking boggart, he is clearly frightened, as he backs away from it. However, when he is able to use the Riddikulus spell, the boggart maintains Snape's body but wears Neville's grandmother's clothes and looks... well, *ridiculous* and much less threatening.

There are ways we can make our scary thoughts seem ridiculous too. Try these out and see which magic combination works best for you.

1. **Repetition.** Repeating a thought out loud as fast as possible for a couple of minutes can make it sound ridiculous. For example, one of my fused thoughts is *"I'm an amateur"* (as in, "I'm not good/experienced/knowledgeable enough). In practicing the *Riddikulus* spell with repetition, I would repeat "I'm an amateur" over and over as fast as possible for 1-2 minutes. After a while, the words blend together and lose their meaning. That is not to say that their implication doesn't hurt, but they might become less impactful after this practice. For this practice to work, however, it will need to be practiced out loud.
2. **Songify.** Another way to make your boggart-like thoughts Riddikulus, is to *"songify"* them – to sing them, perhaps to the tune of a well-known song, such as "Happy Birthday to You" or another song you might know.
3. **Rapify.** A more specific version of *songify* practice is *rapify*. To rapify a thought would be to sing it in a style of a rap song.
4. **Name the story.** This practice involves identifying the themes or patterns in your thoughts, and naming them when they occur. For example, when we have the thought, "I'm a failure," we can name it as "it's that failure story again."

5. **Add a silly ending.** When imagining our worst case scenarios playing out in our mind, we can write a ridiculous ending to such a scenario. For example, if Harry was imagining running into Voldemort, he could also imagine square dancing with him or imagine the Dark Lord trying to ride a mechanical bull while drunk on Firewhisky, and wearing a cowboy hat.

Defense Against the Dark Arts Homework: This week try out the different defusion practices and see which one(s) work best for you. Remember that facing boggarts is not easy, especially when in facing them, we are also facing our biggest Dementors and faced with our most significant and most traumatic experiences. Defusion practice is not easy. After all, it took Harry a long time to be able to apply this advanced-level spell and learn to properly cast Patronus. Give it a go, and keep up your practice even when it's hard. Especially when it's hard.

CHAPTER 8

LOOKING FOR YOUR VALUES IN THE MIRROR OF ERISED

"Happiness can be found, even in the darkest of times, if one only remembers to turn on the light."

— ALBUS DUMBLEDORE, *HARRY POTTER AND THE PRISONER OF AZKABAN*

DURING HIS FIRST year at Hogwarts, Harry takes his father's invisibility cloak out for a "test drive" and finds himself in a dark classroom where he discovers the strange and beautiful Mirror of Erised, which shows onlookers what they desire most. Harry sees his parents and his extended family looking lovingly at him, smiling and waving. This causes him both extreme happiness and deep sorrow since, having grown up without his parents, he desires to feel their love and support. The longing that he experiences is not unlike what we might experience when we too, desperately desire something.

If you were to look into the Mirror of Erised, what would you see? What would you see in the mirror? What would you be wearing and doing? How would you look? Who else would be with you? What other details would be present? What kind of an experience would you see yourself having in the mirror? Take some time to think about this and write it down in as much detail as possible.

When he longs for his parents, Harry feels deep sadness over their loss. However, in recognizing his need for family and by finding his own family, Harry is able to find that which his heart truly desires – a sense of love and belonging. Although he is unable to actually bring his parents back to life, Harry connects with them through his heart and his memories. In addition, he creates his own *chosen* family – Ron and Hermione, the rest of the Weasleys, Dumbledore, Sirius, and the rest of the Order of the Phoenix. Hence, even though the Mirror of Erised can cause excruciating pain to those that obsess over it, it can also be very useful for identifying our core values.

Our *core values* are our life directions, the qualities, beliefs, or principles that guide our lives. For Harry, for example, some of his core values included family, friends, his pet owl, Hedwig, as well as standing up for those who can't stand up for themselves, standing up to evil, doing the right thing, and fighting for the truth.

Core values need to be distinguished from goals. Whereas core values are never-ending life directions, goals are finite. For example, one of Hermione's core values is education, while one of her goals might be to pass her Ancient Runes examination that week.

Our core values can be difficult to balance. Sometimes we put a lot of time and effort into some of them, while at other times, we might neglect them altogether. For example, while she is studying for final exams,

Hermione puts all her attention and energy into her education core value, occasionally ignoring some of her other core values, such as health (by staying up late to study), as well as her time with her friends.

We can think of core values as potion vials. Sometimes, if we put too much time into them, the vials overflow. At other times, the vials might be only half full or near empty. The illustration on page 102 shows two rows of core values vials, each currently represented as "empty." Take a look at these and consider where you currently are with your core values. Specifically, take a look at how much time and effort you are currently putting into each of these core values based on where you'd like to be. You can then shade* in the amount of potion that represents where you currently are in terms of meeting this core value. This decision would not be based on what your family, society, or the Ministry of Magic expects of you, but rather on your personal preference. For example, Arthur and Molly Weasley value education for their children and are not thrilled at Fred and George's decision to drop out of Hogwarts. On the other hand, the twins value playfulness and their career of owning a joke shop over the goal of completing their studies at Hogwarts.

As you are working on this exercise, keep in mind that the exact definitions of these core values are also up to your interpretation, no one else's. For instance, *family* could mean blood-related family, or it could mean chosen family, like the Weasleys are for Harry. Some values might also overlap. Creativity and fandom might both include cosplay or writing fanfic. In contrast, perhaps only fandom includes meeting up with Potterheads, while creativity includes writing music and creating drawings that don't need to relate to fandom.

---

* You can draw your own vials and shade them in on a separate sheet of paper.

For this exercise, identify your own definitions for each core value. Whatever these core values mean to you, the definitions for each are yours, and yours alone.

If you are perfectly happy with the amount of time and effort you are putting into your specific core value (such as *friends*), then you shade the bottle as full but not overflowing. If you think you are spending too much time on your career, for example, then that potion bottle would be overflowing. If you're not spending enough time on a particular core value, then your potion bottle would be less full accordingly, or even empty. Also, feel free to add your own vials to this if there are values that aren't represented. Give it a try now.

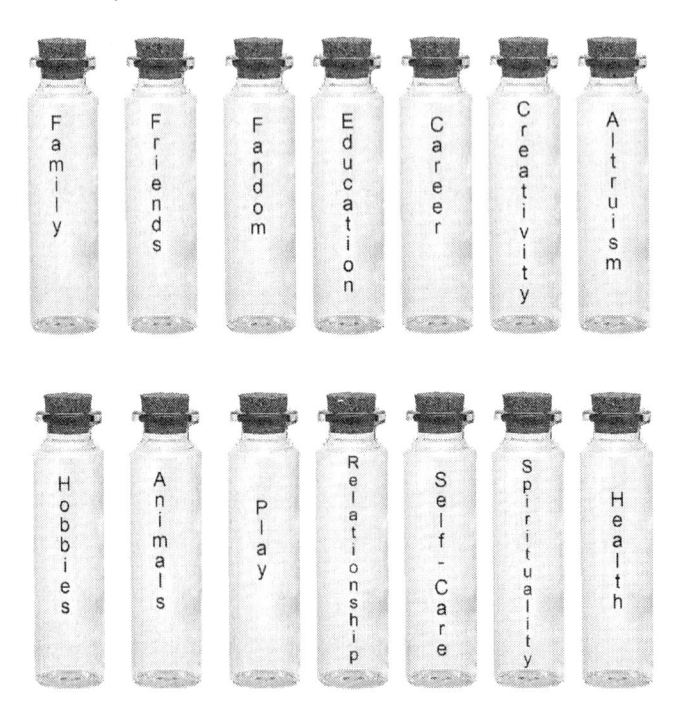

Family	Friends	Fandom	Education	Career	Creativity	Altruism

Hobbies	Animals	Play	Relationship	Self-Care	Spirituality	Health

CHECK-IN

What did you observe? Most people notice that when they first complete this exercise, their values are not balanced. In fact, most people struggle getting *all* of their core values in balance but that's all right - we can always work on adjusting them. Are any core value vials overflowing? Are any nearly empty?

Now let's think of some *very small* goals that we might be able to set for each of the core values that you are not satisfied with. For example, when I first completed this exercise, I was in graduate school. My *Education* core value vial was pouring out, overflowing, while all my other core value vials were nearly empty. Small goals for me meant texting my friends and family, to communicate even if I did not yet have time to hang out with them.

In addition, we can come up with goals which honor multiple core values. For example, playing *Harry Potter* trivia with friends might help us balance *Friends, Fandom,* and *Play* core values. See if you can come up with one or two small goals for each of the core values that are currently not balanced. The goals might be to engage more with the core value, if it is currently not as full as you'd like, or to see if there's a way you can cut down on it a little bit, if you are engaging with it too much.

There are many reasons why we might want to explore our core values. Going through our life without understanding our core values is almost like trying to find your way around the Department of Mysteries at the Ministry of Magic without a proper map. It's not impossible, of course, but it might be quite challenging. Our core values are kind of like the

Deluminator, showing us which way we need to go according to what we hold close to our hearts.

Living our lives in accordance to our core values allows us to follow our heart's path, a journey that is itself the destination. Specific values can differ from person to person. Even Hogwarts houses prize some values over others (loyalty and hardwork for Hufflepuff, bravery for Gryffindor, etc.). Whichever House you belong to, the values you care about the most are your life's adventures. And when you can follow your core values from your heart, that is when you can discover the real magic behind the *Harry Potter* series, just as Cinnamon did.

Cinnamon's story

I am of the generation that grew up reading Harry Potter. I was eight years old when Harry Potter and the Sorcerer's Stone was released in the United States. When the wait for each new book finally came to an end, the midnight release and ravenous reading of the next part of the saga introduced a new season in my life as I began to learn, grow, reread, and reconsider what had come before as I encountered what was new. Even after all seven books were released and many years had passed, I continued, I continue to go back to the series that helped me grow up.

While I can never quite recapture the feeling of reading about Harry, Hogwarts, and the wizarding world for the first time as a third grader, reading the books, even after countless rereads, still leads me up and down on a rollercoaster of emotions. I connect with books, and the characters in books, on such a deep level that I am sure to chuckle, fume and sob throughout. As a person who has experienced death, bullying and trauma, and the depression, anxiety and post-traumatic stress that can arise from such experiences, I usually lack this connection or ability to connect with the real world and real people. As a preteen, books, such as the Harry Potter series, and the worlds and characters that populate them, became my safe haven in a real world I wished to escape.

Luna understood what it was like to be picked on for being different and still embraced her uniqueness and sensitivity. Hermione knew how it felt to be made fun of and used her knowledge to help and protect others. Professor McGonagall experienced so much loss and still remained a brave and strong figure. Professor Lupin knows what it's like to be marked by societal stigma and face personal doubts and still forms bonds with those who care about him.

Each and every character experiences challenges, and many are able to overcome them. After many years, I discovered what is perhaps surprising to some: magic is not the answer to our problems, but rather intelligence, courage, hard work, and even a little cunning can create victory over demons and give us the strength to move on. This means that, despite the fact that I would rather escape my life and go to Hogwarts, I didn't have to live the life the Hogwarts students and professors exemplified.

To me, Harry Potter is a story of love and death. While death is a reality of life that influences all in spite of any attempts to avoid it, love is not a given. The importance of love, described as perhaps the oldest and most powerful form of magic, is the greatest lesson a reader can extract from the series. The ability of love to alter the form of a corporeal Patronus speaks greatly of love's necessity in escaping a swarm of Dementors or a darker depression. It is from Lily's sacrifice of love that saves the life of her son. Love protects life and conquers death. Through love, we can process loss and hurt – and gain new life.

I have not been able to escape all of the dark corners tucked into my intricate brain, but Harry, Hermione, Luna, the Weasley Family, the Professors of Hogwarts, and even Voldemort (whose name I, like Harry, always pronounced), have helped me to destroy Horcruxes created by holding on to death and trauma. Whatever life has to offer in the future, Harry Potter, and the lessons I've learned from it, will be with me. Always.

POTIONS HOMEWORK

See if you can work on one small goal toward one of your core values this week. Don't worry about trying to balance all of your core values at once. Start small, try it out, and see what happens.

PART III
DEFEATING VOLDEMORT

CHAPTER 9

COMMITTED ACTION: FACING YOUR INNER DEATH EATERS

"It does not do to dwell on dreams and forget to live, remember that."

– ALBUS DUMBLEDORE, *HARRY POTTER AND THE PHILOSOPHER'S STONE*

MAY 2, 1998 marks one of the bloodiest days in the magical world – the final battle of the Second Wizarding War, also known as the Battle of Hogwarts. Witches and wizards of different ages and backgrounds stand together and fight against Lord Voldemort and the Death Eaters. They fight with everything they have, using every skill, every spell they learned during their time at Hogwarts. There are many sacrifices but in the end the fight is worth it – Lord Voldemort was defeated, as are many of his followers.

The choices and the sacrifices made on that day assure the future safety for Muggle-born witches and wizards around the world. Surely, many people involved in the Battle of Hogwarts are probably afraid to fight. What is it then that allows them to risk, or as in the cases of Fred, Tonks, Lupin, and countless others, sacrifice their own lives? To me, the answer lies in remembering the "big picture," remembering what this fight is for – freedom, standing up to evil, standing for justice. In a lot of ways it might have been safer to give in to Voldemort's demands. However, I imagine that like the Malfoys, those who would have given in to Voldemort's demands would have regretted it in the end.

It is not the chances we take, it is the chances we do not take that we are most likely to regret in the future. Specifically, if we do not take a chance to do something we care about based on fear, or based on what seems easier to do at the time, we are more likely to regret this decision than if we attempt something and do not succeed. As Dumbledore himself reminds Hogwarts students and teachers in *Harry Potter and The Goblet of Fire*, "You have to make a choice between what is right and what is easy…"

The choices you make might function to avoid discomfort or fear, like the choice that many Death Eaters make in following Voldemort. In the short-term, these choices usually bring relief. After all, you do not have to face the negative consequences right now. However, in the long-term, the decisions based on avoidance of discomfort usually bring remorse and regret.

On the other hand, choices made in accordance to our core values might sometimes be more difficult to make in the moment but they are usually worth it in the long-term. Think of Neville, who starts out as a shy nervous boy in the beginning of the series. During the Battle of Hogwarts, however, he not only stands up to Lord Voldemort himself, he slays the last Horcrux with the Sword of Gryffindor. There is no denial as to the degree of risk that Neville takes, and certainly we do not always need to risk or sacrifice our lives for our choices. However, when presented with an opportunity to stand up to our inner Death Eaters, such as anxiety, depression, or trauma, we can choose to connect with our inner Neville, or our inner Potter, Luna, or other characters you most identify with, and we can choose to make the choice that is most consistent with our heart. This commitment to follow our core values is called *committed action*.

The opposite of committed action is inaction. For example, standing idly by when someone around us is being harassed is an example of inaction. Research studies show that people are more likely to regret inactions as opposed to taking actions even if those actions are not successful. For example, Remus Lupin did not stand up for Severus when the rest of the Marauders were taunting him. He does appear to regret this decision when Harry confronts him about it later in the series. This means that we are more likely to regret not asking someone out on a date, not hanging out with a good friend, and not speaking up for something we believe in than if we were to try and not succeed.

A nurse working in palliative care identified the five most common regrets shared among those who are on their deathbeds. These are:

1. Working too much
2. Not keeping in touch with friends enough
3. Not engaging in enough activities that make them happy
4. Not following their true dreams and core values
5. Not being true to themselves

From these common regrets we might be able to see some similar patterns. That is, people who are more likely to work too hard, not engage in their core values/life directions, and people who don't take chances that they wish they had taken are more likely to have regrets than people who take a chance on what they believe in, even if it does not work out the way they would have wanted.

To be fully honest, I am terrified of publishing this book as I struggle with my own boggarts of "not good enough." However, I know in my heart that I need to release this book in the hopes that it will help others. I hope I will do it justice and I know that I will regret it if I do not take the chance to publish it.

Similarly, Harry's decision to fight Voldemort comes with a lot of setbacks and struggles. However, despite all the heartache that fighting Voldemort and the Death Eaters bring Harry, not following his core values and not standing up for what is right would have been much worse.

YOUR ORIGIN STORY

Let us imagine that like Harry, you also started out having a painful origin story. Maybe like Harry, Neville, or Snape you were also abused or bullied. Maybe like Harry, Ron, or Hermione, you also experience your own fears, phobias, and traumatic experiences. Let us imagine that your pain, your struggles are not the end but rather the very beginning of your origin story, which begin your very own hero's journey.

What if despite your origin, or better yet, *because of it,* you became The Chosen One? What if your fears, depression, insecurities, and traumas did not hold you back any longer and allowed you to live the life you want? In fact, what if there was a *Harry Potter*-like book written about you, in which you are the hero, what would the book be about? How would you like to see the events in your life play out when you are ready to stand up to your internal Death Eaters? What actions would you be taking?

Some people envision themselves spending more time with their friends and family. Others realize that they would like to be able to heal people, while other people might use their painful experiences to help others who are in the same situation. That is exactly what Jill does.

Jill's story

I started getting bullied when I was in 6th grade. I was called "ugly." I was really stunned and hurt. My family always said I was attractive and so did strangers, but at school, I was a total troll. I can remember being at a carnival with a friend. We went into the arcade to play some games. I heard someone say "excuse me" so I simply moved over, to find a kid who snarled, "I wasn't talking to you, ugly"! I went to my friend and we left to find my family. I cried all the way back to them.

When I graduated high school, one of my friends was dating one of the boys who used to call me ugly. I went with her when she had to take his lunch to work one day. She got back in the car and said "He asked me if that was Jill and I said yes, his reply was "Hmm, she used to be ugly."

I went to modeling school to learn poise and confidence as I truly didn't have any. I loved going through modeling school as it did teach me poise, confidence and it really spurred my love of makeup artistry. I'm now a pro makeup artist and I love, love, love my job! I know what it's like to not feel so pretty. When I help another woman see just how gorgeous she is, that is an amazing thing for me.

To those being bullied, if I could give you a hug right now, I surely would. Words can cut just as deeply as a knife but please remember, no matter what the bully says or does, don't you dare let them get to you! I know it's hard and the worst feeling in the world but just know that you are wonderful, you are special and you are gorgeous! I'm sending my love to all of you. Stay strong and above all, know you do have people who love and care about you. They are the ones who matter.

Jill's story is a great example of how we might be able to use our origin stories to help determine our magical path to healing ourselves and others. To follow our core values despite our internal struggles is like using the *Expelliarmus* spell, a disarming charm causing opponents to drop or release their weapons. To follow our core values despite our emotional struggles is to take away the power from our emotions and our past experiences.

We are not what happens to us. We are not our experiences. We are our actions. Sometimes we make mistakes but that does not make us Death Eaters either. It is the actions we choose to take consistently, it is what we choose to stand for that determines who we are as a person. As Sirius Black wisely reminds Harry in *The Order of the Phoenix,* "The world isn't split into good people and Death Eaters. We've all got both light and dark inside us. What matters is the part we choose to act on. That's who we really are."

If all the previous chapters included spells you need to have learned before you graduate from Hogwarts, this step is where you begin to use them to face your own internal Death Eaters in order to live your life according to the book you would want to be written about you.

Committed action incorporates all the previous magical spells you have learned:

1. Establishing your *magical identity* – remembering that you are not your depression, your anxiety, or your trauma. You are *you*. Just like Harry, you are more than one label; you are magical and you make a difference in this world.
2. The Protego Charm of *Mindfulness* – noticing your emotions, as well as your internal and external sensations.
3. The *willingness* to experience painful emotions and memories if they are there anyway. The more we fight them, the more they grow and multiply, like the Gemino Curse in Bellatrix's vault, the very one which caused the treasure around them to multiply, nearly drowning Harry, Ron, and Hermione.
4. The willingness to be *vulnerable* and explore different actions and emotions on purpose, the willingness to say, "I love you" first, the willingness to open up or to fight for what you believe in, like Neville, Luna, Ginny, and the rest of Dumbledore's army do.
5. The *Self-Compassion* Transfiguration – the ability to notice when we are struggling, to notice that we are not alone in our experiences, and allow ourselves to heal and self-soothe, like pouring yourself some cold pumpkin juice when you are dehydrated.
6. The *Defusion* Incantation – has to do with making the boggarts of our anxieties and insecurities *Riddukulus*. Defusion is Ron not

giving into the effects of Slytherin's locket when it emotionally tortures him, and slaying him anyway.
7. <u>*Core Values*</u> Potions – filing up but not overflowing your core values vials. Honoring your core values is like Ron following the Deluminator to connect with his heart and find Hermione.

With these spells in hand, it is now up to you to set up your journey. Review your intention. What do you want to stand for? What actions would you need to take?

For Harry, committed action means protecting Dudley from Dementors. This means the mindfulness of noticing the chill air with an overwhelming sense of hopelessness when the Dementors arrive. It means the willingness to experience these painful emotions rather than trying to run away from the Dementors, as well as following his core values of helping others, while maintaining his magical and heroic identity even in the Muggle world. For Ron, committed action means mindfully noticing his fear of spiders, while willingly facing them if it means saving Hermione after she'd been petrified by the basilisk. For Snape, it means the willingness to be hurt, the willingness to be vulnerable if it means following his core values of protecting Harry to honor Lily's memory. For Luna, it means standing up for what she believes in, even if no one agrees with her.

There might be days when it's difficult to commit to actions that honor our core values, but we can still try. For example, when Ron is angry with Harry, falsely believing him to have cheated to enter the Triwizard Tournament, he still attempts to help him. Even when it is difficult, we can attempt to remember who we want to be and want to stand for. We can be angry at someone and still love them. We can dislike someone and still protect them from danger, as Harry protects Draco.

Just as sometimes we might experience conflicting emotions, our values might sometimes be in conflict as well. There were many instances where Hermione, for example, feels torn between her friendship values in terms of helping Harry find the Philosopher's Stone, and her education core value, requiring her to focus on her exams.

When our core values are in conflict with one another, there might not be an easy solution for how to balance or prioritize them. In these cases, we might need to consider whether one of the core values is more urgent than others and whether we are more likely to regret not fulfilling one or another committed action.

For example, when Umbridge refuses to allow Hogwarts students to learn Defense Against the Dark Arts, Harry is faced with a difficult choice – to teach the students himself and risk getting them into trouble or to keep everyone safe and to follow Umbridge's rules. In this case, his choice is clear – teaching others how to defend themselves against Voldemort and the Death Eaters is more important than trying to keep the students safe from Umbridge. Had Harry not been willing to teach others for the fear of getting caught and getting them into trouble, he most likely would have regretted his choice. On the other hand, even though he and the rest of Dumbledore's Army get caught eventually, this outcome seems to have been worth it in having prepared the Hogwarts students to protect themselves against the Death Eaters.

Value-based actions might not always feel good in the moment but they are an important step toward the big picture. Whether it is spending two minutes exercising per day or 10 minutes working on improving your Quiddich practice (real-life competitive Quiddich or other sports), these are all important committed actions toward honoring your core values.

JOINING THE ORDER OF PHOENIX

This week, let's set out ten goals (large or small) that would allow you to begin your journey of commitment to your core values. These goals could be to purposely ignite your inner Gryffindor in facing your fears, such as to eat in public or inviting someone to hang out if you struggle with social anxiety or to allow yourself to work toward getting on an airplane if you are afraid of flying. Or, you can focus on your inner Ravenclaw in working on advancing your education. Alternatively, you can show off your Hufflepuff pride in being kind and compassionate to others, or you can connect with your inner Slytherin and outline your obstacles and set goals to overcome them. Write out your ten goals on a sheet of paper. Now, write out what would be the cost of you not doing each one (disappointment, regret, missed opportunity, etc.) Now, write out how you would feel if you do complete each one. Each day, see if you can commit to working on at least one small aspect of at least one of these goals.

CHAPTER 9¾

MISCHIEF MANAGED - MAPPING OUT YOUR MAGICAL JOURNEY

"Help will always be given at Hogwarts to those who ask for it."

— ALBUS DUMBLEDORE, *HARRY POTTER AND THE DEATHLY HALLOWS*

Sometime in the mid-late 1970s, while they were still students at Hogwarts, James Potter, Sirius Black, Remus Lupin, and Peter Pettigrew formed as the "Marauders." To aid their mischief, they created the Marauder's Map, which allows anyone using it to track the movements of all beings at Hogwarts.

Though not all of us might know how to use charms to create the Marauder's Map, we can create one of our own, one that charts our own magical journey. We can map out our core values, short-term and long-term goals, potential obstacles, and the pay-off/the benefit of following our goals. For example, among Harry's biggest core values is helping others. His short-term goals during his early years at Hogwarts might be to pass his classes, teach others how to defend themselves, and graduate, while his long-term goal is to stop Lord Voldemort from killing everyone he loves. He is faced with many external obstacles, such as the Ministry not believing him, the death of his loved ones, and simply not knowing exactly how to defeat the Dark Lord. In addition, he faces many internal obstacles, such as worrying about his friends, wondering if he is doing the right thing, and the possibility that he will not succeed. However, the price for not pursuing his core values is too great and he, in different ways, employs all the tools that we learned about.

Along the same lines, someone who values taking care of and healing others might have a goal to go to medical school, for example. There might be many obstacles, which might come up along the way, such as that medical school is very hard and on many occasions you might have a thought, "I am not good enough" or "I am not smart enough to go to medical school." Of course, other obstacles might include the cost associated with attending medical school. The short-term goal would be to take prerequisite classes needed to get into medical school, such as biology. The long-term goals would be to apply to medical school, and possibly, to apply for loans and scholarships.

The table on the next page lists the two examples listed above in terms of Harry's desire to defeat Voldemort, as well as an example of someone who wants to go to medical school. In this case, the core values for both Harry Potter and the person wishing to go to medical school might be the same – to help others.

Value	Obstacle	Short-term-goals	Long-term goals	Skills needed	The benefit of doing it
Help others	Ministry, "I'm don't know what I'm doing"	Finish school	Stop the Dark Lord	Mindfulness, acceptance, defusion, self-compassion, vulnerability, values, committed action	To save people from the Dark Lord

Value	Obstacle	Short-term-goals	Long-term goals	Skills needed	The benefit of doing it
Help others	Hard, "I'm not good enough"	Take biology	Go to medical school, apply for loans and scholarships	Mindfulness, acceptance, defusion, self-compassion, vulnerability, values, committed action	Will be able to help others

Now that you have an idea about how to record your core values, obstacles, and goals, let's place them into your own version of a Marauder's map. The map illustrated on the page below shows Harry Potter's goals and core values, short-term goal (of defeating Voldemort), as well as his obstacles (thinking "I don't know what I'm doing," as well as the physical obstacles posed by the Ministry of Magic). The map then shows the steps (such as using mindfulness, acceptance, and self-compassion) toward reaching his long-term goal (to defeat Lord Voldemort). There are spaces for you to fill in your own goals, obstacles, skills, and core values below. Give it a try and put yourself on the Map.

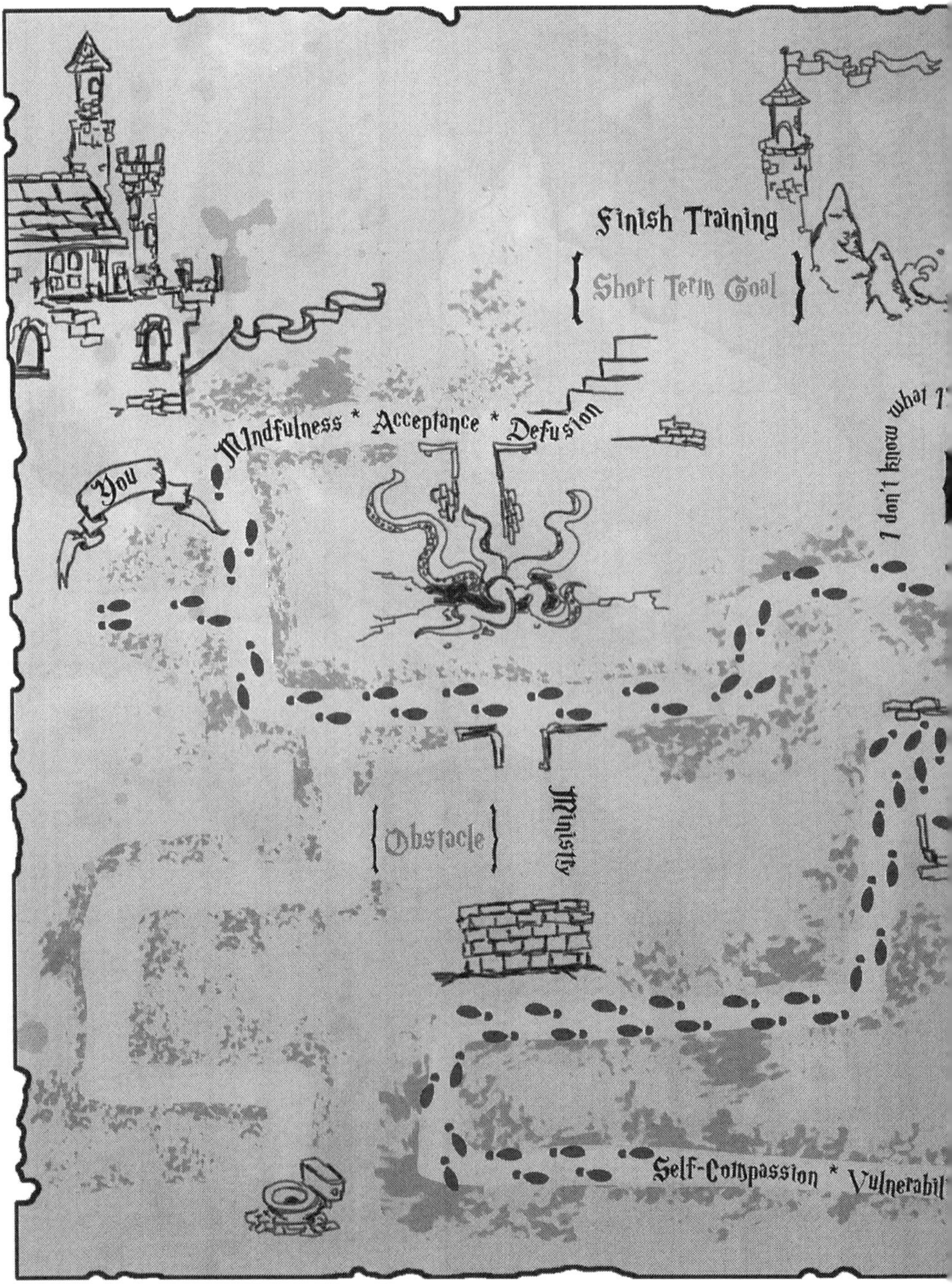
Finish Training
Short Term Goal
Mindfulness * Acceptance * Defusion
You
I don't know what I
Obstacle
Ministry
Self-Compassion * Vulnerabil

{ Value }

the Benefit of doing it

to Save People from Lord Voldemort * Helping People * Helping People * Helping People * Helping People * Helping People * Helping People * Helping People * Helping People * Helping People * to Save People from Lord Voldemort * Helping People * Helping People * Helping People * to Save People from Lord Voldemort *

* Committed Action *

Stop Voldemort

Long Term Goal

ROOM OF REQUIREMENT

After Professor Umbridge makes it impossible for Hogwarts students to learn and practice the Defense Against the Dark Magic, Dobby helps Harry find another room to practice – the *Room of Requirement.* The Room of Requirement only appears to those who really need it.

What if you could use the Room of Requirement from time to time? Dumbledore himself reminds Harry that help is always available at Hogwarts to those who ask for it. Whether it is using the Room of Requirement on the seventh floor, pulling out the Sword of Gryffindor from the Sorting Hat exactly when you need it most, or receiving a few droplets of Fawkes' healing phoenix tears, it is important to remember that when you ask for help in the right places, you are likely to receive it. This might mean asking for help from trusted friends or family. It could also mean getting support from a mental health professional, such as a psychologist or a social worker. Sometimes, we might also need some additional healing potions in order to help us recover. This is where a psychiatrist might be able to help in terms of recommending appropriate medicine.

Keep in mind, just like Hogwarts professors, mental health professionals also are different from one another. If you should ever have an Umbridge-like experience with any doctor, counselor, or a friend, know that just as Umbridge does not represent the teachers and the students at Hogwarts, neither does that person represent every member of their profession. So should that happen, pick up your wand and try again.

Keep in mind that Harry could have never found and destroyed all the Horcruxes, nor would he have been able to defeat Voldemort completely on his own. We all need people in our corner, one way or another and if you are ever struggling, know that there is no shame in that. It is not only okay to ask for help, it is necessary. It does not make you *weak* to ask for help. It makes you courageous. It makes you the leading hero of your own journey.

WATCH OUT FOR THE INQUISITORIAL SQUAD

> *"I suppose that's how he wants you to feel... if I were You-Know-Who, I'd want you to feel cut off from everyone else. Because if it's just you alone you're not as much of a threat."*
>
> - LUNA LOVEGOOD, *HARRY POTTER AND THE ORDER OF PHOENIX*

Even worse than the pesky pixies, are the internal Umbridges, Aunt Marges, and Dementors that might get in the way of your progress. Just like Voldemort himself, our depression or anxiety might sometimes try to alienate us, to cut us off from our support groups. Do not let it.

Notice when there is a pull to seclude and hide away from the world. It is always okay to take a little time to yourself. However, if you are getting to a dark place with your struggles, reach out for help. Like Harry did, allow trusted others to know your quest and your struggles. For example, if you are trying to work on a project but are too overwhelmed with anxiety, reach out for help to your version of Dumbledore, your version of Professor Lupin, or your version of Ron or Hermione.

Often we might find help in the most unexpected places. In addition to entrusting people that we know, as well as mental health professionals, sometimes we might be able to find support online at fan or mental health forums. Sometimes even reading other people's stories allows us to feel more connected and possibly, less alone.

For so many of us, the *Harry Potter* series began as an escape and ended up as a refuge, as a way of finding ourselves, as well as others who might be affected by it in powerful ways. This was the case for Chanteil.

Chanteil's story

I discovered Harry Potter when I was sixteen, a couple years after the books were first released. The first time around I thought it was a good children's book but something changed.

I was living with a Mormon family, which in my view were like the Weasleys. I was the oldest of five kids and instead of thinking of me as just a 'foster child', they thought of me as their oldest. The feeling was wonderful, they actually loved me treated me as a family should.

Acacia, the second oldest, approached me with the first Harry Potter book and said with great excitement, "You have to read this!"

I looked at the book thinking, 'Alright, I'll give it another chance.' That time, I allowed the story to actually sink in. I could understand Harry on a very deep level.

I finished it in a day and asked my little sister to sneak me the second book. I was immersed in the story. Here was a boy who understood most of everything that I was going through and a world that I could actually fit into. I wasn't the weirdo or the odd girl in the wheelchair. Here I was accepted.

That summer I finished all four books in days of reading, after my siblings had read it.

About four months later, I got the news that the family was moving out of state and that meant a new foster home for me. We interviewed family after family, looking for the right fit. Even now, I wish I could have seen the danger that was coming. But how was I supposed to know?

A new family was found and a week later I was to move in with them. That night, I repeated to myself that it would be alright and maybe I would love that family just as much. Inside, I was quite heartbroken but held my head up high in efforts to make the best of it.

I told my new foster mother of my likes and things about me. I told her that I liked the 'Harry Potter' books. However, instead of being supportive she forced her beliefs on me. Then realizing in a way I was placed in the "Umbridge/Dursleys" of families.

From that day on I was told how wicked and defiant I was for reading the Harry Potter books and watching the movies. In those moments I felt alone. There did come a time when the abuse became unbearable, escaping did not work anymore, and when that happened I thought about resorting to suicide, thinking that was my only escape from the abuse and misery.

Having lost all hope, I sat at the bathroom sink holding the razor in my hand and completely prepared to do what I planned to do. One simple thought changed my motives. Would Harry do this? Would he be where I am right now ready to end it all because life had gotten too hard for him? No, he would not because he is a strong, brave, and determined person. His life is worse than mine, in some cases, but he finds the strength to fight through it no matter how hard things get for him. I thought, "I am just as strong, brave, and determined as Harry, so why am I doing this?"

I dropped the razor and left the bathroom.

The story has been very beneficial to me in my own struggles and helped me see that I am worth something. I have made so many friends through the fandom and rediscovered my love for writing by fan fiction. I am very grateful for it.

FINAL TAKEAWAYS

Before closing this book chapter, I want to leave you with a few final notes. First, know that no matter what you are ever going through, you are never alone. There are thousands of others who are also going through something similar and that means that there might be someone who can understand, and hopefully, help.

Second, it might be a good idea to set aside some time every week to review your mental health skills/spells to help you cope with the issues you might be facing that week. This way, you can keep up with your practices.

Third, it is always okay to reach out for help, whether it is to your loved ones or to mental health professionals. Harry does so on multiple occasions and he is one of the most courageous characters in the series.

Fourth, know that set-backs happen. Sometimes we might do well for a while or be able to follow our goals or intentions and then sometimes we might become distracted or something might get in the way. This is completely normal. You can always go back to your practices and keep going. I believe in you.

Finally, I would like to leave you with an enchantment, from my heart to yours:

> "You are loved.
> You are magical.
> You make a difference in this world.
> Always."

REFERENCES

Adams, C. E., & Leary, M. R. (2007). Promoting self–compassionate attitudes toward eating among restrictive and guilty eaters. *Journal of Social and Clinical Psychology, 26*(10), 1120-1144.

Anda, R., Tietjen, G., Schulman, E., Felitti, V., & Croft, J. (2010). Adverse childhood experiences and frequent headaches in adults. *Headache: The Journal of Head and Face Pain, 50*(9), 1473-1481.

Brown, B. (2012). *Daring greatly: How the courage to be vulnerable transforms the way we live, love, parent, and lead.* Penguin.

Chapman, D. P., Whitfield, C. L., Felitti, V. J., Dube, S. R., Edwards, V. J., & Anda, R. F. (2004). Adverse childhood experiences and the risk of depressive disorders in adulthood. *Journal of Affective Disorders, 82*(2), 217-225.

Cohen, R. A., Grieve, S., Hoth, K. F., Paul, R. H., Sweet, L., Tate, D., ... & Niaura, R. (2006). Early life stress and morphometry of the adult anterior cingulate cortex and caudate nuclei. *Biological Psychiatry, 59*(10), 975-982.

Danese, A., & McEwen, B. S. (2012). Adverse childhood experiences, allostasis, allostatic load, and age-related disease. *Physiology & Behavior, 106*(1), 29-39.

Davis, D. A., Luecken, L. J., & Zautra, A. J. (2005). Are reports of childhood abuse related to the experience of chronic pain in adulthood?: a meta-analytic review of the literature. *The Clinical Journal of Pain, 21*(5), 398-405.

Ekman, P., Friesen, W. V., O'sullivan, M., Chan, A., Diacoyanni-Tarlatzis, I., Heider, K., ... & Scherer, K. (1987). Universals and cultural differences in the judgments of facial expressions of emotion. *Journal of Personality and Social Psychology, 53*(4), 712.

Eisenberger, N. I., & Lieberman, M. D. (2004). Why rejection hurts: a common neural alarm system for physical and social pain. *Trends in Cognitive Sciences, 8*(7), 294-300.

Felitti, V. J., Anda, R. F., Nordenberg, D., Williamson, D. F., Spitz, A. M., Edwards, V., ... & Marks, J. S. (1998). Relationship of childhood abuse and household dysfunction to many of the leading causes of death in adults: The Adverse Childhood Experiences (ACE) Study. *American Journal of Preventive Medicine, 14*(4), 245-258.

Germer, C. K. (2009). *The mindful path to self-compassion: Freeing yourself from destructive thoughts and emotions.* Guilford Press.

Hayes, S. C., Strosahl, K. D., & Wilson, K. G. (1999). *Acceptance and commitment therapy: An experiential approach to behavior change.* Guilford Press.

Hofmann, S. G., Grossman, P., & Hinton, D. E. (2011). Loving-kindness and compassion meditation: Potential for psychological interventions. *Clinical Psychology Review, 31(7),* 1126-1132.

Hsu, C. T., Conrad, M., & Jacobs, A. M. (2014). Fiction feelings in Harry Potter: haemodynamic response in the mid-cingulate cortex correlates with immersive reading experience. *Neuroreport, 25(17),* 1356-1361.

Hsu, C. T., Jacobs, A. M., Altmann, U., & Conrad, M. (2015). The magical activation of left amygdala when reading Harry Potter: An fMRI study on how descriptions of supra-natural events entertain and enchant. *PloS One, 10(2),* e0118179.

Hsu, C. T., Jacobs, A. M., Citron, F. M., & Conrad, M. (2015). The emotion potential of words and passages in reading Harry Potter–An fMRI study. *Brain and Language, 142,* 96-114.

Lafko, N., Murray-Close, D., & Shoulberg, E. K. (2015). Negative peer status and relational victimization in children and adolescents: The role of stress physiology. *Journal of Clinical Child & Adolescent Psychology, 44*(3), 405-416.

Lieberman, M. D., & Eisenberger, N. I. (2006). A pain by any other name (rejection, exclusion, ostracism) still hurts the same: The role of dorsal anterior cingulate cortex in social and physical pain. *Social neuroscience: People Thinking About Thinking People,* 169-187.

McBeth, J., Macfarlane, G. J., Benjamin, S., Morris, S., & Silman, A. J. (1999). The association between tender points, psychological distress, and adverse childhood experiences. *Arthritis Rheumatism, 42*(7), 1397-404.

McGonigal, K. (2016). The upside of stress: Why Stress is Good for You, and How to Get Good at It. New York, NY: Penguin.

Mehta, D., Klengel, T., Conneely, K. N., Smith, A. K., Altmann, A., Pace, T. W., ... & Bradley, B. (2013). Childhood maltreatment is associated with distinct genomic and epigenetic profiles in posttraumatic stress disorder. *Proceedings of the National Academy of Sciences, 110*(20), 8302-8307.

Neff, K. (2003). Self-compassion: An alternative conceptualization of a healthy attitude toward oneself. *Self and Identity, 2*(2), 85-101.

Neff, K. (2011). *Self compassion.* Hachette UK.

Poulin, M. J., Brown, S. L., Dillard, A. J., & Smith, D. M. (2013). Giving to others and the association between stress and mortality. *American Journal of Public Health, 103*(9), 1649-1655.

Resick, P. A., & Schnicke, M. (1993). *Cognitive processing therapy for rape victims: A treatment manual* (Vol. 4). Sage.

Rowling, J. K. (2015). *Harry Potter and the philosopher's stone*. New York: Scholastic.

Rowling, J. K. (2015). *Harry Potter and* the Chamber of Secrets. *New York: Scholastic.*

Rowling, J. K. (2015). *Harry Potter and* the Prisoner of Azkaban. *New York: Scholastic.*

Rowling, J. K. (2015). *Harry Potter and* the Order of the Phoenix. *New York: Scholastic.*

Rowling, J. K. (2015). *Harry Potter and* the Half-Blood Prince. *New York: Scholastic.*

Rowling, J. K. (2015). *Harry Potter and* the Deathly Hallows. *New York: Scholastic.*

Rowling, J. K. (2016). *Fantastic Beasts and Where to Find Them: The Original Screenplay.*

Vezzali, L., Stathi, S., Giovannini, D., Capozza, D., & Trifiletti, E. (2015). The greatest magic of Harry Potter: Reducing prejudice. *Journal of Applied Social Psychology, 45*(2), 105-121.

Ware, B. (2012). *The top five regrets of the dying: A life transformed by the dearly departing.* Carlsbad, CA: Hay House.

ABOUT THE AUTHOR

Dr. Janina Scarlet is a Licensed Clinical Psychologist, an author, and a full-time geek. A Ukrainian-born refugee, she survived Chernobyl radiation and persecution. She immigrated to the United States at the age of 12 with her family and later, inspired by the X-Men, developed Superhero Therapy to help patients with anxiety, depression, and PTSD. Her first solo book, "Superhero Therapy" released on December 1, 2016 in the U.K. and on August 1, 2017 in the U.S.

Dr. Janina Scarlet can be found on Twitter @shadowquill, Facebook: https://www.facebook.com/Shadow.Scarletl, or through her website at www.superhero-therapy.com

Dr. Scarlet currently lives in San Diego, California.

Printed in Great Britain
by Amazon